MY NORTH STAR

A POEM COLLECTION ON LOVE, DIVORCE & FINDING A WAY FORWARD

By Chris Statham

Also By

THE UGLY GLORY SERIES

THE MAN IN THE MIRROR - A collection on male mental health
FRIDAY NIGHT FEVER – A collection on booze, nightlife & the battle with sobriety
JELLIED EELS & MULTI-CULTURALISM – A collection on modern life in the UK
THIS IS WHY WE MET - A collection on dating, friends with benefits & sex workers
MY NORTH STAR - A collection on love, divorce & finding a way forward
JUST ANOTHER MARTIAN CAT LIVING IN BASILDON - A collection on exploring creativity & the world
LIFE PRIRATE – A collection on life, death & all that jazz

AFRONIA SERIES

Crying for Afronia (Volume 1)
Escape from Afronia (Volume 2)
Dying for Afronia (Volume 3)
Afronia Rising (Volume 4)
Developing Afronia (Volume 5)

PROSE, POEM AND PICTURES SERIES

7 Days in 1 Week (Volume 1)
12 Months in a Year (Volume 2)
10 Years in a Decade (Volume 3)

OTHER FICTION NOVELS

18 Reflections and 3 Statements of Relief
Paperback Writer

DEDICATION

To My North Star

Copyright and Disclaimer

Author – Chris Statham
Sketches by Hezdean Chinthengah
Published by **www.creativityxroads.com**
My North Star, 978-1-9161867-1-2

CONTENTS

FORWARD

I simultaneously started divorce proceedings and collating my poems; I've found solace in the process. The initial seven years of marriage were filled with the usual ups and downs, this amplified by moving country, cultural differences, having kids, building houses etc. They were generally positive, the last seven less so. It's evident there's need for radical change, this vital for both my ex-wife and myself in order to escape our toxic relationship and salvage a semblance of understanding for the sake of our children. Navigating this miserable process has compelled me to seriously contemplate the essence of the love journey. It starts with hope and excitement before the stress of the wedding and banality of marriage, before the collapse and pain of divorce, all emotions intensified when children are involved.

It wasn't much of a decision to get married, this 14-months after meeting and my fiancé 6-months pregnant. I don't know why I procrastinated; she was my babe, my one and only, my North Star! However, consider this devil advocate's question: are marriages designed to fail? For instance, the elaborate and lavish wedding often exceeds means and fosters unrealistic expectations. Parents, who are seemingly overjoyed at their children's happiness, are simultaneously planning their divorce! Therefore, marriage is a juxtaposition of hope versus disappointing reality. Add in, being in a social media obsessed world where a fuck outside the marital bed is but a swipe away, those who do live married to their dying day are ever more the exception.

If you ask me now, I vehemently argue, that no person can meet all the sexual, emotional, financial and spiritual needs of a spouse, let alone sustain such fulfilment for half-a-lifetime; that's bat-shit crazy thinking, a notion bordering on madness!!And if the worse does happen, why should you not separate? Why does the law of the land try to keep couples trapped in unhappy marriages? Why, when the passage of time and the fading of love are the true culprits, does fault have to be apportioned? Thankfully, such archaic and sadistic practices are changing in many countries, they having adopted a "no fault" option with an even split of assets and access to children. This is far better than catalysing a blame game where children are collateral damage as tempers fray in the ensuing emotional maelstrom whatever the original civil intentions may have been.

As decisions are finalised and papers signed, I strive to find light again and not close my heart so totally that there isn't hope for future relationships. I now realise how vital it is to continually share new experiences in life, laughter and love. That sex and intimacy are a crucial part of marriage, at least from my perspective. Next time, I will go into a relationship eyes wide open— love doesn't guarantee happy ever afters. I am determined to be realistic and not make the same mistakes a second time round.

This collection of poems is a fifteen-year journey from overwhelming attraction to the other's mind, body and soul, having utmost respect and love for each other, to understanding that love is a devotion to an ideal not concrete reality. That the notion of falling in love and living happily ever after is but a fairy tale… but that doesn't mean we should relinquish hope in our pursuit of finding a companion for life's adventures.

THE EUROPHIC PHASE

Have you experienced that enchanting phase of all new relationships, when everything in life is brilliant, a wonderful and vibrant tapestry? When you're in a constant stasis of ecstasy as you've found the only person who truly understands you, whose every utterance should be recorded for posterity because it's so insightful, witty, clever and worthy of preservation for future generations? That time where any blemish or imperfection on their body is wonderful individuality, a cherished feature. When they make you feel like Casanova and you treat them like royalty.

When you're in euphoric love there's nothing you can't do, no hill too high to climb or sea too rough to swim for your lover and newfound best friend. There is nothing that can stop you and nothing you wouldn't do for the other; together, you are invincible. You get the point! When was the last time you were in this state of ecstasy? Did you sneak off somewhere private to confirm this bond of love by having a quickie, an elicit rendezvous? Back in the real world, did you share knowing glances, smiles saying more than a thousand words could ever hope to capture. You know how it is, or at least I hope you do! While the future remains unknown, this is the starting point of a grand adventure as you delve and explore the souls of the other, the future taking care of itself as haunted pasts recede.

My first crush– Fraulein Wachenbach,
my German teacher.
Blonde haired, blue eyed, big breasted;
a teenager's Aryan fantasy.

My first girlfriend– Gemma Philips.
A snog playing spin the bottle the extent of our
romantic liaison.

Older and no girl wiser,
I popped my cherry when 19;
drunkenly forgotten by me,
I forgotten by her.

Years pass,
fumbles in the dark increase,
finding my true love remains elusive.

Another night another barrel of beer.
I spot the girl of my dreams.
We look across the room,

our eyes lock;
is it love or lust?
We don't care as we walk towards the other magnetized,
smiles as broad as the sun;
we kiss and swap phone numbers.

Miracle upon miracle,
we meet the next day.
I'm mesmerised by
her mind, body and
soul,
amazingly,
she likes me...
just for being, well,
me.

We date,
we share a flat,
we rough and tumble
under sheets.

We were in puppy love,
she the most beautiful,
most intelligent girl I've ever met,
I'm the manliest,
most interesting man she's dated.

A year of love flies by.
We take romantic weekends away,
camp and kiss in the mountains,
skinny dip in streams,
party on beaches and dance on tables.

Arguments and laughter had,
shared memories made;
she's my port in turbulent seas,
my life is better with her in it.

I'm in love!
Besotted and bedevilled by her smile,
her mind, her body,
her everything;
I didn't even know I could say these words.

But, I took her for granted as she took me.
Friends and family got in our way,
domesticity became routinely boring.

We drifted apart,
happiness slowly fading,
our love like Icarus flying too close to the sun,
Cherry Blossom's short-lived splendour.

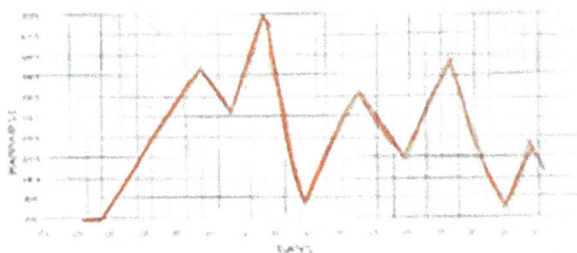

MY GRAPH OF LOVE

Sentences left unfinished,
arguments started over nothing.
Love turned into a growling pitbull.

her turned up lip
once so cute become a forever snarl.

She thought her words were jelly daggers,
but they were sharper and cut deeper than a
Samurai's,
far more than she knew.

I was no longer the person she loved,
I had nothing more to give.
Where once we were in love,
now I just loved the memory of us.
Where our love was once a luxurious blanket,
tattered rag destined for the scrap heap of life it
became.

Animal magnetism was all that kept us together,
life, a tumble-dryer of love,
hatred,
love,
argument,
hatred... only hatred.

We were shadows of who we were,
memories of love hovered like a laughing cloud;
our love was broken beyond repair,
there were no more tomorrows.

That was two years ago and now when I look out
my window,
I see parched ground,
the grass brown,
the rains not coming,
no sprouts of life,
hope.

There are plastic flowers in a vase.
the irony of indoor colour;
this unreality is love futility.

I want to change the world,
the rules of what's possible,
the plastic flowers a sad allegory,
I, lying to myself.

My life is a desert,
void of affirming water,
plants and people die caught in my web,
a death spiral,
destruction my defacto,
regression,
compression,
suicidal depression—
is this the best way out?

And then I met you,
was it 6 months back,
7?
8?

You were a silver lined cloud on the horizon,
the bringer of hope,
joy,
a new start in the cycle of life.

There was some kinda connection,
neither knew where it might go.
We swapped numbers,
but most likely two ships in the night,
a brief flirtation,
before immigration,
accepted resignation,
noting to do but contemplation.

We kept in contact,
fate waved her wand,
happenstance happened,
the mysterious of the universe stayed mysterious,
somehow,
in lands unknown,
we are to meet in hours,
soon to be minutes.

What will happen?
Will we click,
light switch flick,
possibly it'll be sick,
awesome,
long-time stick or maybe...
you'll think I'm a prick?

Those months of communication now minutes,
the future yet to unfold,
the train of destiny has left the station and will
not be stopped.

I get dressed up for this night of destiny,
nice shirt,
fancy shoes,
full of swagger;
this, my last chance saloon.

Pay my dollars,
buy my drink as I wait,
wandering if tonight I'll set the dance floor on
fire.

Enter the bar,
ready for clubbing.
It's sweltering,

I'm sweating,
I'm watching,
the DJ playing great tunes,
bodies pressing next to mine…
but not the one I want.

I feel the revellers heat,
their sense of being alive,
as I keep searching,
hoping to see you.

I look across the room and see my woman danc-
ing like there's no tomorrow.

I catch your dazzling eyes-
which world will they lead me to?
What new chapters will be unveiled?
What experiences of the heart,
body and mind will we share?

My heart leaps,
trepidation of the unknowable,
excitement of a possible future together.

You drive me crazy,
yours locks now cut to the skin,
so alive,
so sexy,
so confident,
this the ultimate aphrodisiac,
you the centre of attention,
the one who all the boys want to be with;
will you be mine?

What was unsure became sane in minutes.
Connection confirmed on the motorbike riding
pillion,
I touching your black pearl,
the massage with your mouth in the taxi on way
back.

We have a relaxed Sunday,
fish not spaghetti,
walk sunshine and music,
film always a happy-ending;
life seemed natural.

Both have difficult situations,
your understanding mine,
I hopefully inspiring,
guiding,
provoking,
helping you to change,
to be your true self,
to live temet nosce.

We met a second time on foreign soil,
you eloping with lies.
There was so much chatting,
joking,
sauna and shower sharing,

steam-room fucking.

And when the sun rising,
our bodies slick from the summer night,

I see your body glistening,
nipples pointing to the stars.

Hands explore as sweat encrusted bodies reunite,
joined at thrusting hip.
We rumble in the jungle,
my thunder to you lightening,
I'm a volcano you a tornado,
trembling in unison.

We hold each other,
whisper sweet nothings before you shimmer to
the bathroom,
towel rounds hips,
hourglass shape,
breasts perky,
moving like a lioness comfortable in your naked-
ness.

You rub down,
bends over,
dries toes,
shows great ass.

Pick out what looks good and pull down dress
I tell you,
no panties, I'll slide my finger into your wetness.
You smile coyly,
undresses,
crawl back on all fours for more playtime.

We don't know how the future will play out,
I might not have plenty but I have you,
a badass by myside,
a fellow life pirate not afraid to take on challenges
unknown;
we have an invincibility others can't understand,
are jealous of.

Months go,
ups and downs our new show,
roundabouts and squabbles,
this expected in a relationship bubble.

Some get out of hand,
but we are together…

is it forever,
fate intertwined,
we super-glued?

Captain Morgan is our drink,
pork and rolex our food,
weed our smoke,
rugby our sport,
laptop our work,
fun and freedom of mind body and soul,
our default.

Often drunk,
horny,
getting high,
dancing in the bedroom,
staring into the sky.

We live free,
take overnight coaches and sing karaoke,
met friends and laugh about shithole hotels.

We shag like rabbits…
in the bedroom,
before getting changed for a night out.

First thing in the morning,
before going to work.

In the kitchen,
while preparing a romantic meal.

In the nightclub toilets,
we can't wait.

Behind the bike sheds,
like a school crush.

In the garden,
the thrill of being seen.

In the sitting-room,
bent over chair…
where others sit.

On the stairs,
to try it everywhere.

In the bathroom,
while others are watching TV.

In the car,
just like the movies.

In the stationary cupboard,
the office relationship cliché.

In the aeroplane toilet,
to join the mile-high club.

In the sea,
in view of sunbathers.

With others…

Last night of a holiday was one for the memory
bank,
you,
my 8 fingers,
3 times before breakfast anal queen,
experienced for the first time pussy eating,
titty sucking,
finger banging,
bed wetting,
clit nibbling,
with our bi friend,
this, the climax of the adventure!

A wonderful time never to be forgot,
stories told to siblings and friends,
memories to consider while waiting,
wondering,
where and when we will next meet again,
what adventures are waiting to be had.

That was four months before,
now we are into our third act,
a long distance relationship.

"But I would walk 500 miles,
and I would walk 500 more
just to be the man who walked a thousand miles
to fall down at your door."

So the Proclaimers sang in their 80's pop classic.

Being with someone
but a distance apart-
a pure torture.

I can't smell you…
when you're sleeping in another bed.
Hear your laughter…
apart from down a crackly phone line.
See your smile…

other than in photographs.
Only able to share a joke…
on Skype.
No romantic dinners,
but meals for one.

I can't feel your body pressed next to mine so
hug a pillow.

You, my lover,
best friend,
partner in crime,
sixth sense who knows what I'm thinking,
one word confirming our mutual understanding.

Long distance relationships—
apart but together.
Having too much time to think,
to turn mind in knots.
This is neither the love of partnership nor the
freedoms of singleton life.

Being absent from my
lover a pure torture;
I have the need for
intimacy
but no one to be intimate
with.

I am here you're there
life separating us,
but this is loving.

I think about you,
want you,
but you're out of touch.

Two hearts separated by oceans,
one life split by circumstance.
We are together,
in spirit if not body.
in same hopes and dreams,
of remembering past times,
good times,
loving times.

We can't know what the future will bring,
if we will reunite or be apart,
reconsumate or share beds with others,
fate deciding our forever,
memories our past.

Separation can make the heart grow stronger or
take it to breaking-point.
Long-distance relationships,
the worst of both worlds as frustration builds up,
longing for the touch of another body,
whisper of lips,
mind and soul rejuvenated,
makes mind fucked-up.

But tonight we reunite,
five months have passed and this is date night,
I'm high as a kite,
the world of shite,
months of separation soon to be forgotten.

Tonight,
I'm with you,
my lady,
my missus,
my lass,
my sister from another mister,
my bird, bitch,
maybe one-day baby mama,
soulmate,
my everything in life,
maybe future wife???

You're showered,
smelling sweet,
smooth to the feel,
looking airtight,
a princess as you head into the night.

Razor to my face,
iron to the trouser,
comb through hair and a splash of aftershave.

I leave the house feeling good,
looking forward no more backwards,
no regrets,
only hope;
together,
forever,
two as one.

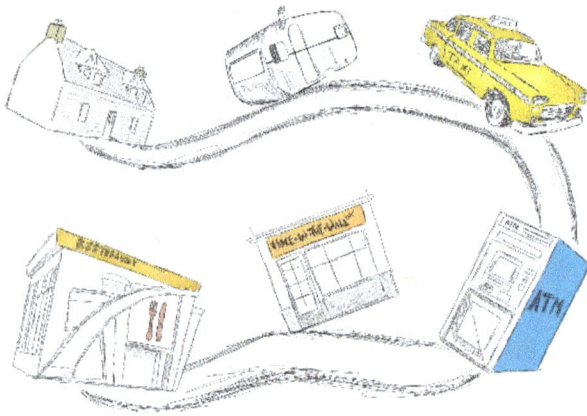

Jump in a taxi,
visit an ATM,
go to a bar,
down a shot,
tonight we'll set the dance floor alight.

15 minutes 3 seconds
since left home,
restaurant I approach,
you looking fine and we're about to dine (on
love).

That was last night,
this morning I watch you as the moon fades,
the sun rising,
our bodies slick from the equatorial night.

Cocooned under mosquito net
our bodies glisten,
my hands run over your body,
yours over mine.

You smile,
your sexiness enrapturing,

body tight,
wet.

We reunite—
lips locking,
hips thrusting,
love and lust,
two minds in unison.

Once in the pussy,
once in the ass,
once in the shower…
naked breakfast.

We are fucking,
sucking,
making love
so elemental to who we are,
so needed for a peaceful heart,
there is no point pretending.

Sex,
how we are conceived,
where life comes from and emotions lead,
companionship and intimacy central to the hu-
man condition,
something we can't live without;
when we're screwing this is life connecting,
not faking.

You allow me to be someone I am free with,
who I don't want to pretend with,
who I always want to be with.

THE WEDDING AND HAPPY MARRIAGE PHASE

Is she the one, the love of my life? I asked myself. I don't know what Grace saw in me, but here comes some self-analysis… for all my flaws I'm authentic. You get what you see; I'm not a fake aspirational advert. Maybe, I was her life-raft from a desperate situation and the first person to give her a smile of friendship rather than leering glance of desire or sneer of lust? I simply don't know. It's impossible in a short space of time to know if we would thrive as a couple, as lovers, as best friends, as soul-mates; only time holds that answer.

My grandmother once shared a wisdom with me: marriage is like a pair of shoes— if they are comfy you can go anywhere; if they are the wrong size you'll always be plagued by pain. What I realise after nearly 14 years of marriage, is, that in a world where we are told to conform, to fit into shoes that are either too big or small, that you must find the courage to stand out, be different and sing from your own hymn sheet. To do that, you must hope to find the partner— the pair of shoes— that fits perfectly. Accept that you are an individual with plus points and many flaws. If you're lucky enough to find a partner in crime, embrace them. You will squabble. You will break-up and have make-up sex, passion-ate reconciliations. Humans are the most irrational of rational beings. Accept this truth and cultivate honesty with each other.

That day we met,
I was dishevelled,
disinterested,
despondent—
steam from a coffee cup my only friend that
frigid day.

I was mentally exhausted,
shattered even though no long day at work,
no studying from home.

I was unemployed
unemployable,
unlovable,
lost in the sea of life,
in an ocean of depression and floating aimlessly.

Whisky was my companion that desultory,
inflammatory,
revelatory night when your smile,
your comforting voice offered companionship
and meaning to my life.

You are and always will be my muse,
my North Star,
my Mona Lisa.

You with a heart of gold and a thousand stories,
with dimpled cheeks,
flat stomach and a squeezable bubble-butt.

You are the embodiment of vitality.
radiance and energy,
a real firecracker who lives the mantra:
today not tomorrow;
if not now, when?

Your lust for life, despite the challenges,
inspires me to be a better man,
partner and lover.
You saved me,
you gave me a reason to keep living.

I was foolish before with women,
but hope I'd learned from mistakes.
All I want is you,
your body next to mine.
Your soul,
so we can be partners .
Your passion,
to match mine for you.
I believe we're meant to be together.
You're a tornado and I a volcano and we will
witness disasters and triumphs,
but together,
we can create.

The truth is,
we are two brains one soul.

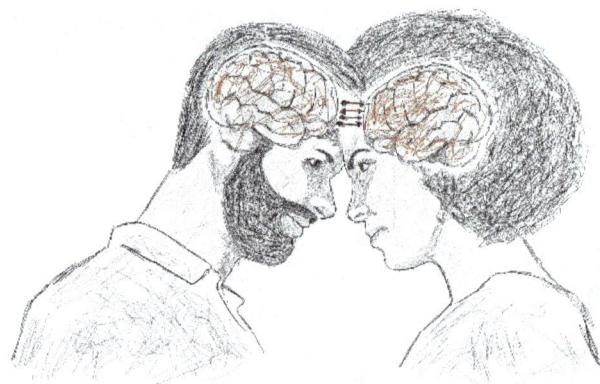

I've been bitten by a donkey,
that was a funny story.

I was bitten in hatred,
that was grimmer.

I've bitten much food,
that's mostly been tasty.

I've been bitten by love,
and I loved getting bitten by you,
Grace.

You are my one and only,
my friend, my mate, my pal.

We argue, we cry,
we have make-up sex.

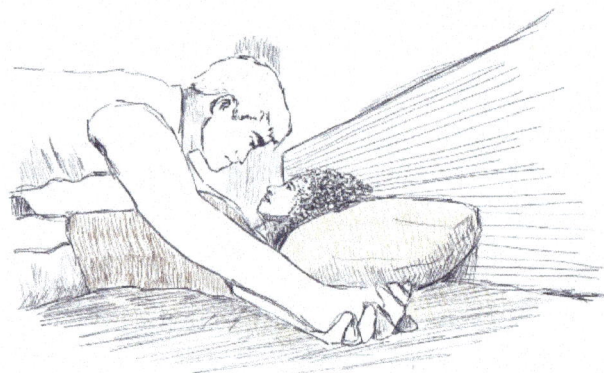

You know me better than I know myself.
My strengths and weaknesses,
you accept.
My foibles and annoyances,
you tolerate.

16

We are stronger together,
please,
let it be forever.

As we go forward we need to have the big discussions now as who knows what the heart wants.

Let me articulate my principles for a good marriage,
as while lust infatuates,
this will be replaced by the ordinary,
the everyday;
we must be together on the big questions!

If life has told me anything,
relationships start with sex and end without getting any.
Whether boredom,
repetition or lack of novelty,
what was once fresh dies on the vine.

We must make a conscious effort to keep it spicy,
to agree sexual boundaries,
what we like or don't,
whether to live with limitations or expectations,
to be open about fantasies,
fetishes;
we can make them all reality.

We already had a threesome,
hope this reduce jealousy,

insecurity,
while increase openness,
freedom with each other.
If one of us takes another lover,
keep it safe,
respectful;
we must talk to each other about experiences and emotions.

Money is the root of all evil,
the source of most conflict,
the water that can split the rock,
the source of poison if things go wrong.

Each should be financially independent.
One will always earn more than the other,
but the other will contribute more meaningfully in other ways…
Everyone likes surprises,
big or small from someone's hard graft,
from their good heart.

Kids or no children?
If, yes, our life will be upturned;
they are the truest form of pure altruism,
one will do anything for them.

They are a joy,
a financial burden.
We must get ready for physical and emotional ups and downs;
there is no getting away from these truths.

These are some of the big discussions,
we need to have sooner than later,

before kids,
before marriage.

We must understand core principles,
beliefs,
check we are aligned on the major issues.
If we are, the details will take care of themselves,
mistakes will be made and forgiven quickly,
understandably.

Do we agree on our religious understanding?
If there is or isn't?
Agree the boundaries and expectations,
not one-dimensional recommendations,
we coming from different starting-points.

These are some of the discussions,
our soon to be every day,
questions that will make or break us,
better we have them before we get oven-baked.
Grace,
I'm sitting here thinking of the future,
thinking of you,
my love.
I contemplate life as I investigate your sweet
smile and hope for more tomorrows.

I consider the choices I've made–
the years gone by,
the loves lost and found,
the times I've danced to the tune of life and
others missed,
due to choice.

Choosing A rather than B,
going to X and not Y,
meeting F…
and falling in love with G,
Grace.

Choice,
sacrifice of the alternate,
one not necessarily better than the other,
but different.

What I know,
I don't look at the paycheck
but what we have together,
love.

Two halves make a whole,
one without the other we would both be weaker,
unfulfilled,
not reaching our potential.

Love is like an unrestrained fire that can't be
contained…
we can't be stopped if we have each other.

In life,
we make choices,
are responsible for decisions and accountable for
actions;
this is what it means to be alive,
why I'm so happy to be with you.

I might not be a square-jawed,
six-packed millionaire,
but there is no other man like me,
someone unique,
who can and will give you so much more.

I understand your pain and hopes as I too suffer
and take risks like you;
there is no one who will give you as much as I.

Nothing is impossible in my world.
While others might have more materially,
they only have half the heart.

You can be free with me;
there's no need to trick or deceive.

I want you to live your life,
one of freedom.
freedom from judgement,
freedom from the fear of failure and questioning,
freedom from fear itself.
When you ask, does someone have my back?
I always will.

I am someone who understands your every fibre.
I love you for your freedom,
your transparency,
that you live your emotions and don't try to hide
them.

I hope you're happy,
that your glad we're together,
that we allow the other to thrive,

to live life secure in our partnership,
neither one trying to best,
to beat or control the other;
we are collaborators not competitors,
lovers.

And now that day has come,
a time I never expected to see again,
not just for affirming my love,
nor what I hope for tomorrow,
nor a break from my past,
but an absolute satisfaction in the present,
with you.

I've been waiting for you,
Grace,
all my life.
Today, we have only hope in front,
regrets, fears, and insecurities in our rear-view
mirror.

I've searched for many a year to find my port,
you,
my North Star has guided my soul to a safe haven,
from where I,
will take you to worlds unknown.

This is the day when I promise,
together means forever.
Where,
I commit to love you in sickness and in health,
richer or poorer,
to forsake others…
unless you,
my lover,
allows.

This is a day when two halves become one,
when broken pasts change to hopeful futures,
when we are made whole,
completed by the other.

As we progress through turbulent lives
we must believe, trust,
honour and respect each other.

We should be humble in our love
and not suffer from pride.
We must accept each other's frailties,
forgive weaknesses and revel in combined
strengths.

This day,
is the day I've been waiting all my life;
I couldn't be happier marrying you,
my North Star,
my forever Grace.

As we walk into the future
we can't change the past,
but must live in the present.

Last night two became one;
from those two,
maybe more will come?
Together,
side-by-side we march forward,
hand-in-hand towards the horizon,
ready to take on any challenge,
knowing life is an adventure,
a rollercoaster of emotions and experiences,
smiles and tears;
this is the essence of life.

You and me live life large,
free,
we don't live to others rules,
society's limitations and expectations;
we are roundheads not cavaliers.

Children we have,
Christmases come and go,
New Year fireworks explode,
photos taken.

You know me,
always having a dance,
a jig,
laughter and fun my middle names.

I catch an eye,
a pretty girl,
but no fatal attraction,
spunky,
but she's getting none of mine.

I advance and extend a hand,
grab her waist,
make some twirls,
salsa,
dance and flirt.

There's no harm no
foul,
all is good in the
world,
I have no animal lust for her as she's not my girl,
not my New Year,
not my future
not my Grace.

You and me live life large,
free,
we don't live to others rules,
society's limitations and expectations;
we are roundheads not cavaliers.

This is who we are,
individuals and together,
doing what others can't even think.
When we play,
punch is playful.

Fucker,
said with lustful eyes.

Bastard,
hate not in words.

Maybe?
Hope expressed.

Kiss,
this time not chased.

Hands,
exploring.

Skirt and shirt,
lifted.

Zip,
undone.

We reunited…
at the hip.

We are lovers,
forever.

Pain is temporary.
together forever.

We can put arguments in the past,
have a mutual peace offering:
a restaurant date;
no friends,
just us two.

We go to the fanciest spot in town,
not been there before,
but first stop,
a hole in the wall.

We enter,
ushered to our table,
candles are lit,
very romantic.

Open the menu in trepidation…
the food sounds yummy…
as it should be at those prices;
service charge and VAT not included.

Do I choose what I really want?
A quick calculation,
not enough money in my skyrocket.

Grace,
at times you're oblivious to my financial distress
so order the lobster,
champagne;
are you testing me?

I bite my tongue,
I daren't spoil the night.
I have buffet,
a reasonable price—
glass of wine for free.

The food is tasty,
we're not disappointed.
My mood soured when I see the bill,
then lightened when I see your sweet smile.

A trip to the fancy restaurant,
best friends again,
love re-engaged!

Ours a love boomerang,
as when I sleep you're always in my thoughts,
my dreams.

We,
a life of perfection,
you my butterfly,
I your lion.

Our aspirations,
entwined into a life of one.
Me as you,
you as me—
together,
forever.

Together,
two in one,
hope for a bright tomorrow,
for a life never apart.

Joy and despair
we will share.
Laughter and sadness,
we cry together.
Success and failure,
our joint future.

You are me
as I am you.
We'll tackle the world together and nothing will
break us,
shake us,
nor split us.

You are my madam.
my mate who holds my soul.
We are the reflection of the other,
our future in front,
the past behind.

We live for the now and I live for you.
You, who give me courage,
hope and your love.

Love that I need,
crave,
and friendship I desire.

I'm your companion.
I'm here to heal your
wounds;
I'll be your doctor, nurse and
therapist.

We are Humpty Dumpy,
but there is no need for sol-
diers nor all the king's men,
our love is whole and we will put each other
together again.

We have done so much,
more adventures to come,
taking risks,
sometimes failing,
life never boring,
often irritating,
frustrating,
done too much recent contemplating.

We are circles,
glorious orange globes.
We might not,
don't always fit into the square of society's expec-
tation,
lack of imagination.

We are not that person,
that image
that perfect four equal sides in a culture that
castigates,
need to validates
not always tolerates
as they try to mould us into something we are
not,
cannot be,
our true self,
someone to appreciate,
drink and date,
live life,
not regurgitate,
depreciate.

When we see opportunity,

excitement,
we go full-throttle,
120%.

Ours is not a life of wondering,
boredom,
9-5,
but to give it a go or die trying,
regrets for another day,
this is why,
how we see links,
life,
through a different lens;
no and impossible,
not words for us.

Being a circle,
a human not robot,
we challenge others',
squares perceptions of who we are,
what someone can or can't do.

We face our own challenges
insecurities,
learning how to live in this world as the 1 %,
but we understand each other,
live happily in each other's orbit,
reasoning,

rationalizing,
we are more together,
1+1=3.

We have arguments,
disagreements,
this normal in all relationships.

Sometimes ask,
can it work?
Can we make it work?
You wanting more than I can give,
you offering less than I want,
this leads to battle,
mind rattle.

When we are in a bind,
we work out how to break that stick,
so always move together not apart,
depart;
I don't want our love vanishing like a fart.

We are people who live large,
take on and conquer.
We need to remember who we are,
That we have free minds and open hearts,
not walking on eggshells,
pretending to be someone else,
being mice when we are lions,
conforming to be squares when we're circles.

This is what will should celebrate,
venerate,
if freaky, ejaculate,
but no more eternal commiserate.

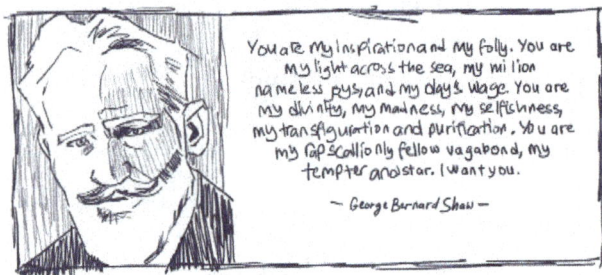

You are my inspiration and my folly. You are my light across the sea, my million nameless pussys and my day's wage. You are my divinity, my madness, my selfishness, my transfiguration and purification. You are my rapscallionly fellow vagabond, my tempter and star. I want you.

~ George Bernard Shaw ~

You and me live life large,
free,
we don't live to others rules,
society's limitations and expectations;
we are roundheads not cavaliers.

You still help me hit my high.
With you in my life I'm always scoring a goal,
winning a contract,
writing creative gold,
getting a hole in one.
You are the girl of my dreams–
this is my nirvana,
you the elixir of my life.

Until I know what got me high I settled for the norm,
the ordinary in life…
but you showed me how to strive for the un-
known,
aim for the stars,
live the extraordinary,
dance the night fandango,
be a king for a day;
fulfil destiny and reach for my zenith.

Together we climb the nearby hill,
it doesn't need to be Everest.
Cycle to the local shop,
we don't have to be Wiggo.
Start a business,
even if not entrepreneurial dragons.
Help the needy,

with a kind action, word or deed,
as what's ordinary to you,
us,
maybe extraordinary to others.
as it's not the size of the achievement but the
quality of the change,
the living of the experience,
of reaching your potential and achieving your
target.

And that's why we're here together,
to see,
to dare,
to challenge,
to know what's possible,
to find out what we're capable of,
to know what motivates us,
to live the life we desire.

I just ask,
don't be jealous of others,
as what floats one boat might sink ours.
Don't live life by others' rules,
but understand ours,
each helping the other to hit their high.

As birthdays come and go my dear,
I pray for your happiness,
that your wishes come true as you blow out candles.
I say, excel in not knowing what surprises lie in
wait,
what joy and heartache we will experience in the
year to come.

When I wish you,
happy birthday,
know, I will support you to make your dream
comes true,
be by your side through the journey of life.
Two more powerful than one.
One,
bringing two together;
we are still true love

Its seven years on from that night of destiny.
We didn't say,
I will, in front of a priest,
but that's what our hearts told
each other.

Six years ago,
two became one,
and from that partnership,
two more arrived plus one.

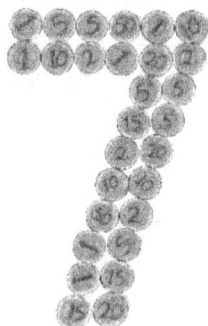

We've had time together and apart,
doing what we need to keep our dream alive,
for our future no matter obstacles or challenges.

Life is an adventure,
a rollercoaster of emotions and experiences.
Through good times and bad,
we've cried tears of laughter and sadness,
but always together.

Happy anniversary.
Here's to seven more years as we march forward
side-by-side,
hand-in-hand,
towards the horizon,
ready to take on any test,
together,
forever,
Living life as cavaliers not roundheads.

THE, WHEN IT STARTS TO FALL APART PHASE

Long-term relationships, marriages never unfold in a straight-line, never; that's pure fantasy perpetuated by Hollywood. There will be peaks and troughs. When you think things are going well, something will bite you in the ass. To keep matrimonial harmony, try to laugh about it, sort it out and then move on together. Remember, never sleep on an argument and, that you never know where you might find love but when you do hold onto it dearly and don't mind what others might say behind your back.

The simple truth, is, that the everyday is what I valued more than short-term adrenalin rushes fuelled by alcohol, drugs or chasing skirt. Mowing the lawn into a little football pitch. Having a picnic in a forest. Getting the kids ready for school is what gave me pleasure. I think, this is what they call domestic bliss. It's only losing it all that I appreciate what I once had, the true value of life itself.

My advice, life is never easy, so find humour in any situation, work through the challenge together and move forward hand-in-hand.

I must confess, during the hard times, I started questioning if together meant for ever. Would love and infatuation run its course? What would happen after the come-down? At times, I contemplated, why should I limit my love to one person? I didn't go beyond thinking into implementing, but admit, at times I was on the cusp as our relationship inextricable moved towards the proverbial deathbed.

The life I've lived,
the person I am,
Grace, you taught me many lessons.

From distress,
you were my rose,
the person others wished to be with.

You are the one in a hundred,
who never said, never,
who doesn't take a backward step,
for whom I would walk 500 miles…
and 500 more.

Work takes me away from you,
us.
I'm with you in mind but not person;
don't let distance destroy us.

People talk but I don't listen,
my replies,
half-hearted;
it's too long since I've seen you,
held you,
kissed you my beloved.

I've travelled,
been home alone,
thought, but didn't share beds with ladies of the night;
I've never found someone to cuddle,
to make me laugh like you do.

I've enjoyed peace,
quiet,
hedonism,
different experiences but now I want home,

to be guided by my North Star
to safe harbour,
to lay my head next to yours.

I want your smell,
to hear you quietly snore,
your laughter,
to see your smile light up a room.

For us to share meals and memories.
To eat every part of you as I run my tongue over
your body.
To feel your heat as we sleep together.
To share our sixth sense,
the other completing our thought.
To share a look of understanding
rather than turning mind in knots.

Being apart from you,
is killing me;
Grace,
my love,
please forgive my impulsiveness
my impishness.

Weeks away continue passing,
been boring,
life sleepwalking but Friday night coming,
should be entertaining,
dancing,
reuniting
flirting
hopefully lead to us finally fucking,

Then I get your phone
call…
it's whinging and
whining,
insinuations making,
incriminations
threatening,
it's a moan calling,
bitchy calling.
a deliberate,
try to make me lose my vibe calling.

Why can't you be happy?
Where's you joi de vive?
Why not live carpe diem?

You don't always need to be introspective;
life can be joyful.

When we met you were a stranger;
I didn't know if you would be the love or pain of
my life.

There was kissing of lips
running hands through hair,
of sharing jokes under duvet.

We dated,
we made plans;
you're the love of my life,
I couldn't contemplate you ever being the pain in
my life.

Marriage bells rang,
hope was eternal,
we understood each other,
partners in crime.

Kids we procreate,
parents cremate,
generations come and go
we part of shared history.

Anniversaries pass,
domesticity ensues,

love turned to wanderlust;
you became the itch of my life.

When we first met
hands would explore,
but we locked that
door and now lie
back-to-back.

Secrets are kept,
beds not slept,
living different lives,
telling multiple lies.

You are never here,
your body I can see,
but your heart and soul in distant land.

Voices are raised
hearts dashed,
no more amazed.

Tempers flown and fists thrown.
dreams crashed,
hope smashed,
friendship bashed.

I'm heartbroken.
You were the only love of my life,
now you causing me so much soul pain.

I'm not willing to accept the truth that your heart
is gone,
never to return,
our love forever broken and yet we are still two
in one.

We have a shared past,
a painful present,
an uncertain future;
you are still the love of my life,
the pain of my life…
please don't become a ghost in my heart.

We can hope for a future
where we reveal our past and share the present,
where we pass time together rather than time
passing us by

There is still love…
a key to unlock the door,
once more to explore and lips reunite.

You are the love of my life,
the pain of my life..
You are my life but being in love with you is like
an amateur darts player,
I aim…
but don't know where the arrow well hit!

We used to make love in a tent,
partied on beaches,
kissed up mountains and danced on tables.

We have shared memories,
arguments and laughter.
I still love you,
my valentine.
you,
who I know so well,
now I so many drinks,
over thinks.
living together is hell.

I finish a fridge full of beers,
a shelf of hard stuff as all I think of is you,
your smile,
it's been a while.

I need a person that makes me feel good,
complete with myself,
with life,
with the world I live in.

Someone so I stop feeling alone,
a fucking clone,
a person who lives in a shadow,
not being who I could be,
should be,
don't have the courage to say,
fuck you, bae!

I'm caught in a trap,
like a rat,
our marriage now nightmares and dramas,
my mind Bananarama,
AK-47 and Everest death zone.

But,
somehow we survive,
carry on,
two still more than one,
together painfully forever.

Happy valentine,
my wife,
this such a sad life,
our hearts now apart.

I am still me,
who else do you want.
me to be?

I'm a circle,
a glorious orange globe,
you're a triangle
full of angles…
you want us to
fit into a square,
a cube of
expectation,
this too much
imagination.

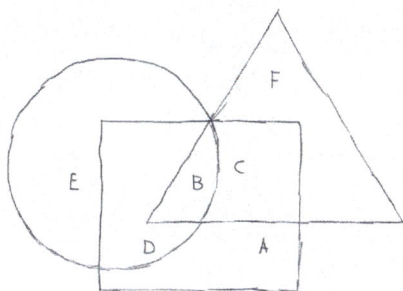

You castigate,
vilify,
no longer tolerate,
try to mould me into something you can obliter-
ate not.

My true self,
who you have forgotten,
thrown away,
is when I'm not with you,
maybe with someone else who can appreciate,
drink and date,
live life,
not abate,
depreciate.

Sorry than I'm not that person,
no longer that image,
that perfect for you,
but I am me,
don't like walking on eggshells
pretending to be someone else,
someone I'm not,
a mouse when I'm a lion,
your insecurity and jealousy,
killing all that was good with us,
obliterating lust.

We are in a bind,
so how do we break that stick?
Move on together or apart,
depart,
our life that had such promise now vanishing like
a fart,
but we still have a chance,
if we can both accept,
adjust.

I'm a circle and you triangle,
let's stop trying to fit into a square,
but celebrate,
venerate,
if feel freaky ejaculate,
please,
no more eternal commiserate,

as while we got married,
still are hitched,
the reality,
I feel like a floundering singleton with a wed-
ding-band.

We are birds of a feather,
two in one,
the other knowing us better than ourselves;
this attracts
frustrates,
emotionally constipates.

Our marriage is painful,
too much anger,
sometimes joy,
more often love dissipate.

You are a tornado to my volcano,
I never know when or where the next grenade
will go of,
the next twister to destroy the calm,
change the scenery.

We are creative and destructive forces
shape shifters,
givers of life after annihilation.

We have a life,
kids,
dogs,
but we live in a house not a home.

We are not happy,
both trying to find a way forward,
I for one, failing.
The lack of dirty weekends,
fun nights out,
doing anything together,
killing me.

You're a snowstorm,
I a tsunami.
You're a blanket that smothers,
kills by a thousand wounds,
I batter,
but from destruction comes new light,
new ideas and beginnings,
not always fight.

We are reality changers,
re-arrangers,
nature and nurture,
humans who do things,
make own rules,
others,
mere mortals,
9-5ers,
Mr Mortgage and Mrs Pension,
can't imagine much less dare.

But, there is a black hole of jealousy,
insecurity;
nothing good can ever come from it.

It's not controllable,
but overwhelmingly destructive,
nothing created,
time always wasted.

This is not sustainable
winnable,
all very disagreeable…

but somehow we still together,
somehow,
I think,
hope,
we have more together than apart.

There is too much negative energy,
fighting;
imagine if we were back in lock-step,
same goal,
direction,
like before,
lots of create.

We are forces of nature,
positives and negatives amplified in unison or
fight.
Together,
in alignment,
stronger,
two in one,
but,
god help those caught in the maelstrom,
they collateral damage to our ego,
our id.

I still love you,
my tornado.
Nothing is impossible when we push the same
direction,
emotional energy dilated when we point in oppo-
sites,
our relationship,
all or nothing,
fire and ice,
a lack of spice and killing souls.
We are the masters of our destiny;
no marriage is perfect,
I don't know how much longer ours can last!

We can decide our own rules,
not what others,
what society decides,
dictates.

Love is not a rules-based system.
We don't have to accept the norms but can live
free-minded,
rejoice in our success and failures,
for this is what we pass onto our children,
the ability to choose,
to make a choice how to live.

You're a tornado,
I volcano,
together we've created four.

But you are making me so angry and confused
mad,
as I'm rejected,
ejected from your life,
but you still fabricate on social media,
selling a dream that's turned regurgitate.

I'm angry and confused,
what do you want?
I'm not made of stone and loving you hurts.

Every conversation,
discussion turns into argument,
heated and shouty,
you must always be righty,
never compromise,
agree.

I'm angry and confused,
what do you want?
I'm not made of stone and loving you hurts.

Every restaurant,
hotel,
holiday and present is never good enough;

you refuse to do it,
always easier to criticise than compromise.

I'm angry and confused,
what do you want?
I'm not made of stone and loving you hurts.

You say,
you don't know how to do some things,
that you can't.
you don't have experience...
but it's pure laziness,
controlling,
always wanting,
expecting others to do your bidding,
to bow down before the queen bee.

I'm angry and confused,
what do you want?
I'm not made of stone and loving you hurts.

You throw my work back in my face,
but you don't know what you want.
You have choices built on our sweat,
but it doesn't mean you can have it all;
decide your priorities and stick to the plan,
the grass not always greener on the other side.

I'm angry and confused,
what do you want?
I'm not made of stone and loving you hurts.

You've sowed confusion,
apprehension through your self-determination,
generations,
older and younger,
no longer sure of what we're doing...
neither am !.

I'm angry and confused,
what do you want?
I'm not made of stone and loving you hurts.

I'm no longer man of the house,
final decisions mine to make no more;
you have taken this responsibility,
but can't accept accountability;
the crown doesn't sit easy on your head!

I'm angry and confused,
what do you want?
I'm not made of stone and loving you hurts.

You have killed me,
us.
My heart is ripped out,
it's better I give it to someone else than put it in a
dark hole.

I don't know how to move forward by myself,
with you,
with hope,
I fear life will repeat itself.

I don't know what to believe when I can't believe
anything,
when we are so far apart,
don't communicate.

We are in a quandary,
of that it's certain;
it's time to close our love curtain.

Neither sure how to move forward,
what is the right direction?
We have a love,
but now scrapping the mental barrel,

afraid of the unknown,
mourn for lost dreams rather than celebrate what
we have achieved.

When something is wrong for you,
it's wrong for me to,
we,
mirror selves,
the ying and yang to the future,
happiness of what might be,
now sadness of the could have been!

All I can say-
it's enough,
it's enough,
let go of your mistrust,
stop hurting me,
us.

We had such smiles,
hope,
expectation,
not constant reflection,
deflection.

It's enough,
it's enough,
let go of your mistrust,
stop hurting me,
us.

What's happened to openness,
past histories to be laughed and commiserated?
Why are we falling apart,
away?

It's enough,
it's enough,
let go of your mistrust,
stop hurting me,
us.

Our love is tinged by reality,
uncertainty,
infidelity,
lack of unity,
no soul responsibility,
too much accountability,
pride before humility.

It's enough,
it's enough,
let go of your mistrust,
stop hurting me,
us.

All that was sweet has turned sour.
Our heat,
frozen.
Our relationship,
alive but no longer living,

It's enough,
it's enough,
let go of your mistrust,
stop hurting me,
us.

We reminisce of yesteryears rather than thinking
of tomorrows.
We can survive,
but this is not thrive like we used to.
What's been lost…
can it be rediscovered?

It's enough,
it's enough,
let go of your mistrust,
stop hurting me,
us.

I cry for the what ifs,
maybes and perhaps,
knowing what has been said,
done,
decided,
can't be reversed,
expunged.

It's enough,
it's enough,
let go of your mistrust,
stop hurting me,
us.

Relationships come and go,
hope crushed,
smashed,
bashed but get back up again,
this part of life.

It's enough,
it's enough,
let go of your mistrust,
stop hurting me,
us.

My heart collapsed,
I'm emotionally trashed,

doing what I need for sanity,
protect mental fragility,
that would be finality.

It's enough,
it's enough,
let go of your mistrust,
stop hurting me,
us.

You are hurting,
so am I.
We take it
show it,
shake it in different ways,
anger or escapism,
time and positivity can lead to love revision.

It's enough,
it's enough,
let go of your mistrust,
stop hurting me,
us.

Our choices are written in history,
destines designed,
fate waved her wand when we met.
What will happen next,
how life will unfold,
where you and I will be,
I cannot tell,
ours a story of dreams dashed,
star crossed lovers,
ships that met in the night but got smashed in the
safety of port.

It's enough,
it's enough,
let go of your mistrust,
stop hurting me,
us.

Remember,
we were two in one,
I thought together meant forever.

We had one voice,
same vision my love,
my dear,
my soulmate,
the mother of my children,
where are you now,
where am I?

We describe what we do,
not how we feel,
our differences more than similarities.

You seem more concerned with who you know,
your likes on social media
rather than what's best for our family.

We rarely do anything together apart from paying
bills,
instead we walk on eggshells for fear of raised voices.

We don't go for weekends with the kids,
or just the two of us–
rarely even a restaurant.

You happily say,
you're a no sex person,
but it wasn't always like this.
You won't countenance an open relationship…
but I have my needs,
I still have appetite.

We take the easy actions,
the ones with least friction rather than having
tough,
engaging conversations to address problems.

We are bound in a marriage contract,
not of love,
but handcuffs,
emotional blindfolds,
bound together with
brambles,
responsibilities,
love and empathy no
longer our bond.

We are talking but not sharing,
describing not melting,
no longer friends but business partners,
our love like wearing uncomfortable shoes.

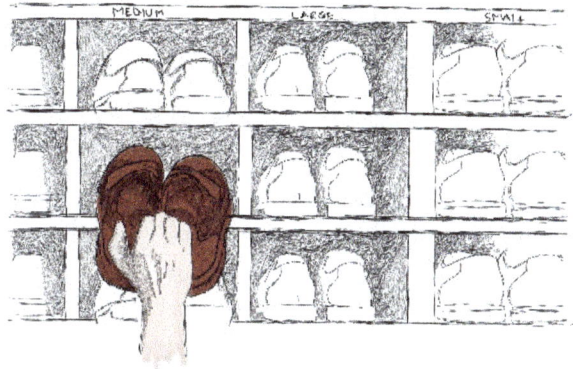

We have roles and responsibilities,
familial out of duty rather than love,
you,
my lover, gone AWOL.

I'm lost to in-decision and unhappiness.
We living two lives with no singular direction,
no more shared dreams.

There is no soul between us and little mate left.
We are lives intertwined,
kids that we procreate,
bank accounts we share,
our love,
once unbreakable now little meaning,
highly fragile,
a piece of paper,
a legal bond all that keeps us together.

Time has dimmed the light fandango through
complacency,
commonality,
domesticity.

You say you love me,
but that doesn't mean what it once did,
what I still want.

I'm confused, lonely and lost.
I feel no love for you or from you.

We have a shared past and live unhappily in the
present;
do we have a future?

This is a poem of emotional distress,
redress and sadness,
I no longer know who you are,
who I am.

Are you a diplomat,
businesswoman,
housewife,
all the above,
none of the above?

Who are you,
what is your identity?

Why don't you want to be my lover,
my friend?

You have it straightforward,
never had to struggle,
not that there haven't been struggles,
but you've done what you want,
when you want…
it seems,
you no longer want me,
so what do you want?

I've tried,
but seems I've failed.
Find out who you are,
what you'll fight for.

You think I'm like everyone else,
no longer shaping the sun or the stars in the
night sky.
You doubt,
take for granted the extraordinary in an ordinary
life.

I sacrificed for you
was happy to do so,
but it's never enough,
you always wanting more.

Why can't you be honest with me?
Why do we no longer anticipate,
experience and find exciting each other's passions?

I want to feel desired,
air attired,
fired out a cannon,
alive,
living,
being with a female,
a tigress;
you no longer woman enough.

Just be honest,
transparent with me.
We're both human and you are my everything;
I only want your love.

Do you remember when we first met there was
such honesty,
openness.
We loved each other in the present
despite our messy pasts we had such hope for a
future was as no secret too big to hide,
no truth that couldn't be told.

Suddenly,
life made sense.
Your words of wisdom answered my questions
about life and love;
you, my salvation,
I, your port in stormy seas.

We had fun,
we would frolic.
The days were too long when apart,
the nights too short;
we were in love,
nothing could break us.

Time passed,
love grew stronger,
plans longer,
belief in us deeper.

Months increased to years,
passion turned into friendship.
love into parenting,
time was not ours as we built a future for others.

Accusations start flying,
time by self, grew longer,
white lies more frequent,
loathing replacing loving.

So, I ask you,
what is truth when truth you don't know?
If life is a lie,
is that living?

You want me to change,
to grow up,
to stop seeing my friends,
spend more time with you…
I wanted you to stay the same,
all smiles,
my best friend.

I've not changed,
or so I think…
but now I'm told,
I'm not responsible,
accountable;
you have become incomprehensible.

No longer am I good enough,
don't treat you well enough-
in all ways…
I'm not man enough.

And so now we are here-
we had everything,
now nothing,
only the kids keeping us together.

Where truth brought us together,
the pasts our glue,
deception now drives us apart.

Constant deceit,
past arguments and indiscretions are the drugs
that clogs our veins with concrete,
our joint soul in retreat as we stumble,
tumble,
frequently rumble,
rarely show humble our marriage unfolding,
imploding.

It's true,
we no longer glue,
you, the female of the species from Venus…
I from Mars,
you now as incomprehensible to me as a pineap-
ple to a hamster…

You talk rough for a woman,
act tough for a woman,
are strong as an Amazonian…
but cry like a little girl.

So much anger leaves me perplexed,
I'm the hamster staring at a pineapple,
you still an earthquake to my tornado,
our life and love,
volatile;

the good was amazing,
but this bad, devastating.

We live 100 miles an hour,
surrounded by noise;
now,
time for calm,
joy and fulfilment.

We both need peace,
as where once there was love,
now,
I just love the memory of us.

We've hurt each other too much and too often.
I've forsaken passion with others,
forsaken fun with friends,
adventures—
you took all these from me
but still want more.

I have no more love to give;
you've drained me as I've drained you.
Do we have a future?
I don't know,
I can't tell,
but I'm not willing to yet split,
to cut our umbilical cord.

I still believe,
have hope,
we can somehow make it.
But now we both need peace,
appraise what we've lost,
decide if we want each other,
if there's still love.

You talk rough for a woman,
act tough for a woman,
are strong as an Amazonian…
but cry like a little girl.

THE AFFAIR – THE LIGHT IN DARKNESS PHASE

It's a helluva conundrum, a perplexing conundrum how to keep relationships loving and interesting. Certainly, both partners must work at it, a real joint effort. Good sex should be a reward for doing good stuff with your partner rather than as a right. In a way, this roundabout statement reflects the enduring bond that kept Grace and me together through the tumultuous times, despite the hurtful words and actions we inflicted upon each other. It speaks to the underlying connection that persisted, even when tested by adversity. However, in any sort of relationship there comes a breaking point, in the case of marriage, this often means, or should that be results in infidelity. After all, why have a takeout burger if there is steak at home? And besides, in different times and cultures, it was perfectly acceptable, normal even to be polyamorous.

lingerie lonely sex partners dinner families excuses love consider cheat divorce husband conversation married hotel

ADULTERY

intercourse sexual guilty affair consequences wife romance sneak fling affect extramarital lies spouse women

What a week,
what a life,
what a bunch of cunts.

Now do own thing,
love gone,
accept a life of up and downs,
emotional coaster,
that's how I roll.

Rough with the smooth,
wins and losses,
hope meet good people on the way.

New city,
new life,
same trouble and strife,
wife,
old problems,
conspiracy and girls,
mainly in the imagination,

always exaggeration,
emotional constipation,
messing what was good.

Meet friends,
chat nonsense,
chat work,
no twerk,
all guys doing our business,
serious…

When come home,
where there was love,
lust,
that now lost.

You want me to be this,
assertive,
you want me to be that,
passive,
coercible;

make up your mind,
who do you want me to be?

I longed for your love,
but you gave me sex calendars and I made excuses.

Tell me, no,
I say, yes!
We used to dance,
groove to the music of life.
We were as one,
now move alone.

Life can make you cry,
other times you're flying in the sky;
don't over analyse when fate is the future.

Grace,
you wish upon a star that we go to the UK,
but I warned you,
be careful for what you wish as you might just get
it!

We moved,
not to the Promised Land but to hell and back.

Remember,
playing with a toy gun can get you killed!
A pet can bite you!
A car you can crash!
A lover who will try to change you!
A new country equals new problems!

You think the grass is greener on the other side,
but it might just be a small patch in a desert of dust.

Settle for what you have,
for me,
be mine again, I pray.

Endless questions run through my head,
am I still important to you....
Why?
For what?
What do you need me for that you can't do your-
self?
Money, is that it?
I feel no love otherwise you would hear my cries,
you would share you hurts and hopes once more.

When I'm away,
working,
bringing funds for our family,
you treat me like shit,
like I'm nothing.

I'm so unimportant to you that you can't call me,
reply to my messages when I'm asking for your
thoughts…
not even a voice message from the kids.

Really,
I'm important to you?
You show me I'm such a hassle,
your actions speaking louder than words,
this killing me.

You have made decisions,
decided not to share thoughts,
show no videos or photographs of our children;
I'm no longer an active part of your life,
only financial benefits;
there's nothing left.

Don't you remember that we were friends,
lovers,
crazy motherfuckers?

Nothing could stop us,
get in our way,
impede or imprint their will on ours.

We moved to our rhythm,
did as we pleased,
made life, our bitch!

Rules were there to be broken,
rewritten,
moulded into our form.

We were impetuous,
decisive,
not caring about the consequences.

That was then,
this is now,
both still crazy,
able to do what others can't imagine while we
rush headlong in.

Why did you lift us up to shoot us down?

I'm no bad boy,
a piece of rough,
but a normal guy,
living a normal life,
with normal heartache.

Why did you lift us up to shoot us down?

We met at a bar,
I was your brother's friend,

sex was on your mind
I, putty in your hand.

Why did you lift us up to shoot us down?

We shared a shower,
sneaked around like James Bond,
times never to forget.

Why did you lift us up to shoot us down?

These were good times,
we equally up for anything times,
a few drinks,
a bit of flirting,
always time for skinny dipping,
then I dipped into you,
once,
twice,
thrice.

Why did you lift us up to shoot us down?

The younger me,
the one full of spirit,
didn't know how to treat a girl,
love a girl,
be confident with a girl;
I was an amateur,
you taught me how!

Why did I lift us up to shoot us down?

The second,
older,

more determined me,
loves going different paths;
I full of confidence,
purpose,
but this not enough for you.

Why did you lift us up to shoot us down?

You were the desire of my life,
the making of my life,
a fantasy wife;
why did you take me as a fool,
crush and betray me,
our love?

Why did you lift us up to shoot us down?

You were my one and only,
my soulmate.
We had a life of regretted pasts and hopeful
futures,
that made us instant click,
connection.

My did you lift us up to shoot us down?

We shared,
two lives destined to be one.
A love,
understanding,
that I always dreamed of,
was always frightened of;
I went all in,
not thinking of losing.

Why did you lift us up to shoot us down?

You lifted us up then held a shotgun and shot us
down?
I hear it in your angered voice,
the fake news that you still love me.
in the taste of your tears of self-pity,
your angered face.

Why did you lift us up to shoot us down?

I smell your new perfume that you wear to please
another.
I feel the whiplash of your shunned back and
taste spittle when you shout at me.

Why did you lift us up to shoot us down?

I feel it in my heart the distrust,
the hate and contempt;
our relationship now ruined core,
of a life together finished.

Why did you lift us up to shoot us down?

Why did you shoot us down?
This, the first question I ask myself,
the next,
was I... the bully,
who threw insults and fists?

Was I... the narcissist,
who knew everything about anything?

Was I... the manipulator,
who went from kiss to kick in a heartbeat?

Was I... the liar,
even the kids know this answer?

Was I... a skirt chaser?
Not even 2% of the rumours.

Was I... the breadwinner?
You better believe it!

Am I... crushed,
my heart broken in pieces?

Am I.... frustrated,
I only wanted a friend to be open with?

Am I... still hopeful,
for you, me and brighter tomorrows?

Am I... excited?
With others I can be,
you no longer excited by me.

Am I... sexually frustrated?
Yes,
what do you honestly expect?

Am I... your soulmate?
We once were.

Am I... anything to you?
We both know that answer.

Am I... still a parent?
That won't change to my dying day!

Am I... a regretful person?
Not for the life we shared!

Am I... angry?
only of the, what could have been.

Am I... a sexual deviant?
You were never willing to experiment.

Am I... a rainbow?
I'm not a black and white,
a, yes or no,
right or wrong person.

Am I.... a wild card?
We both are,
this our essence?

Am I... a volcano?
You were my tornado.

Am I... excitable?
We all should be;
this is life,
we only have one!

Am I... close to the edge?
Why have you pushed me so hard for so long?

Am I... a mind-reader?
No, but you seem to think you are.

Am I... a person with friends?
You seem determined to break them.

Am I... close to my family?
So, so. I don't pretend otherwise;
why are you trying to break those bonds?

Am I... a jealous person?
I train myself not to be,
I wish you would also.

Am I... anything to you?
Not anymore,
not for a long time.

Am I... the one who hates you,
or is it you who hates me?

Am I.. annoyed?
Yes.
We have done,
could still do so much more together.

Am I... rejected?
by you I am… and it's difficult to look beyond
why you reject me,
us,
our shared history,
our shared experiences,
our family.

You,
who prefer to be right,
to fight,
always one-dimensional correct,
your decision final,
no compromise or communication.

You,
who never admits mistakes are made on both
sides.
You,
who doesn't want a future together,
but apart,
for me to depart,

to be alone,
rejected,
dejected,
no longer lusted after when erected.

Will I... be the only adulterer?
I doubt it.

Our life,
friendship,
marriage,
has creaked and cracked,
splintered and breaking apart.

Why?

We had a life together,
if not perfection,
I was your lion and you my butterfly.

Our aspirations were entwined into a life of one—
me as you, you as me—
we thought,
together meant forever.
That,
joy and despair
we would share.
Laughter and sadness
we'd cry together.

You are me and I am you.
We can still tackle the world together,
two more powerful than one,
together should be forever.
I truly believe that nothing can break us,
shake us;
I still want you by my side.

Take me or leave me,
accept me or walk away;
love me or hate me,
the choice is yours.

With choices comes decisions,
accountability,

responsibility,
mother-fucking reality.

I want freedom and stability,
all the women in the world...
but only loved one good'un,
experience serendipity,
find happiness and make others happy.

Life is a menu of choices,
what do I choose?

I'm lucky,
fortunate,
made my life how it is,
choices and chances my burden,
my joy,
my cornucopia of irony and opposites,
is this the world I want to live in?

When I sit and watch,
listen and admire friends,
I see they reach,
achieve,
be who they are,
who they want to be...
honest...
living their true selves.

They sing of passion,
love...
as they have excitement in each other.

I look on happy and sad....
happy for them,
sad for me,
we,
I full of love jealousy,
barely hanging on.
I cry tears of loss,
sunshine of rays, happiness,
now clouds of hopelessness.

Friends,
lovers together enjoying being in each other's
company.

I can't help but be jealous of times I no longer
have,
of the passion void I inhibit,
a missing part of the human psyche.

Why can't I be them,
travelling,
adventuring,
exploring the world and each other?

It's hard to be happy
when others are having fun,
when I feel single even though married.

I have to be disciplined,
accept my life is different,
that I still control my destiny.

I remember compersion
to be accountability for my choices.
This sounds fine,
but it's a dividing line,
a real mindbender.

I can't sleep,
trying too,
war on the news,

turmoil in my mind,
nothing sits good.

Work a stress,
marriage no connection,
erection;
life is jam sponge.

Reasons for this reality
a history of calamity,
emotional criminality,
can't just be banality,
need vitality.

Your body I can see,
but your heart and soul are in distant land.
How can I hope for a future when you don't
reveal your past or share the present?
We are passing time,
as time passes us by.

Knock, knock, knock on the
window,
Gone past one,
been sleeping since fell asleep,
go to investigate,
strange but familiar drunk face I
see,
talking nonsense...
all coincidences now making
sense–
your boyfriend,
toyfriend,
don't know what else to say.

We talk and talk,
try to understand,
no hypocrite me.

No jealousy or anger,
finger-pointer,
each, our soul laid bare;
an honesty we didn't have before.

This is fucked up,
changed up,
not what expecting life leading here.

Tricky no doubt
but better this than more lies,
deceit,
search thru purse for hidden hotel receipt,

That is not living,
being true,
but living under a cloud of lies doesn't work,
the heart wants what it needs,
a power that is indestructible,
unbeatable.

Better honesty,
accept reality,
take risks,
have trust and hope,
find solutions,
be open-minded.

No more restrictions or moral superiority,
understand life is messy,
only the resilient survive then thrive.

Maybe fall down but never stagnate,
this is life,
an unending cycle of hope and happiness,
regret and disappointment,
positivity and negativity,
giving a shit then things get fucked-up.

What do I want now,
this time in my life,
a missing wife?
What makes me get out of bed,
feel motivated,
fully anticipated,
not constipated,
castrated?

I need love, love, love-
we all do.

That special one who will pull you up when down,
make you smile when feel like crying,
remind you that tomorrow is another day,
who knows,
the tide might bring in new opportunities.

A someone to join my adventure,
to keep my wanderlust in check,
to not let boredom become destruction.

A someone together to explore new lands and languages,
smells and girls,
tastes and temperaments,
life,
always an education.

Someone who will test me,
thrill me,
excite and motivate me,
someone I can feel pride as a provider.

I want more sex,
to give and receive pleasure of every sort, no limits;
try everything once, my motto.

I want a woman,
a motivation to get out of bed,
feel pride in what we do,
to have adventures with as we journey through life,

who will encourage me to cut down booze and increase exercise.

A woman who I can support as she supports me,
who will make me cry in happiness
thankfulness and not sadness,
loneliness.

I also want fun,
with a hun,
someone to take away stress not add to it.

So, fuck you,
screw it,
one life,
live it,
bad news,
bin it.

I'm only me,
moi,
a calculated risk-taker,
life maker,
not commuter,
but communicator,
explorer,
fun ambassador.

Stop fucking me around,
be honest,
anything possible,
we can make open-relationship work.
This doesn't mean sing to our own tune,
dance alone,
but both look for another crazy soul.

We search in this life for a soulmate,
you a friend gone,
don't become an enemy I thought we could ever be.

Life,
moving one day to the next,
trying to get through as best we can,
lonesome and loveless,

careless with mind, thought and body,
just wanting oblivion.

I will wake to a new sun,
look for a new Ms Crazy...
you're my life…
don't want you anymore to be my wife,
a nagging bitch,
start fighting for nothing;
I don't get it.

Why do you think annoying me can help,
honestly?
That madness,
a bottle of wine, on it.

Think I'm going to be rationale,
sentimental,
no, I'm emotional,
hormonal,
want to rebel-
fuck your shit!

Into the night I will go,
women on my mind,
fate,
I, in her hand.

I will keep my options open,
this what I have been reduced so worthless do I
feel.
I'll search for hope in the hopeless,
feel defeated,
hated, so go on dates.

Will this be destiny,
more heartbreak,
futility not sexuality?

I want a new mind
body unexplored,
someone who I want to know,
who interested in me.

Someone who could become my girlfriend,
build that physical and mental bond with,
our lives,
our bodies join,
two becoming one,

A girlfriend,
a woman to educated me,
remind me to live,
that life doesn't stay still,
to appreciate what I have,
when and who I have it with.

And then it happened,
Like how I met you my soon to be ex-wife,
no longer my life.

With Safire,
our lives,
our age,
our everything so different.

I'm a horny old guy,
she a beautiful young woman-
this a cliché,
each getting what they want,
drinks drunk,
spliffs smoked,
fun times had.

I'm loving the now,
have own shit to contend with,

worry about,
kids and a wife,
a life that I loved,
but seems no more for me.

Responsibilities,
I was happy to shoulder,
but I also need joy.
I want more than bitterness in my life,
kiwis not just lemons.

And Safire,
starting life,
hope,
the joy of youth,
limited experience,
waiting to see what comes,
open to opportunities,
seeing someone,
me,
who can help her.

I'm ok with this,
fortunate to choose,
to support,
to take advantage,
this not an even relationship,
both knowing the truth no matter what the chemical,
biological reactions might be,
all I want is your honesty,
brutal reality,

I've had enough secrets and lies,
duplicity,
it's too much complexity,
my mind went spaghetti.

Safire,
my new crazy that I want to be with,
spend time with,
who makes me feel good,
whole.

I'll wait for you, Grace;
are you coming back to me?
As for now,
my eyes are locked,
my lust unblocked with Safire in my arms.
Our bodies shimmer,
hips thrust,
my lips no longer dying of thirst.

Safire has found my mind and unchained my soul,
like you before,
she makes me whole,
her Ying to my Yang.

Grace,
My dear,
We've been married 14 years,
monotonous 11,
monogamous 11,
hate filled and depressing last 6,
fun,
not a lot.

I'm on the edge,
heartbroken,
soul drained and lawyer called.

Kids as unsure as I of the future,
but this misery,
insults and conspiracies,
fists and shouting,
is not a way to live,
it has to stop.

Minds are made up,
no more emotional blackmail,
don't beg or insult,
but if you open your mind maybe your heart will
follow?

Life is for living,
exploring and experiencing new sights and
sounds;
I want sensory overload.

My dear,
you will always be close in my heart not matter
the barbs,
but what you offer I no longer want.

I want laughter not lectures,
a common direction and respect not each doing
their own.
To appreciate efforts and not be taken for grant-
ed.
To realise, one person can't meet all the needs of
another,
no matter dents to pride.

I do not own you or you me,
our marriage,
when it comes to it,
just a piece of paper.

I will not drown in your bitterness,
be gobbled by your anger and hate.
If you want a way forward,
accept, now is the time for three,
four in our relationship…
or divorce.

This is the reality,
you,
my wife,
love of my life,
soulmate and spirit,
who knows me more than I know myself and I
you.

We're had too many times shared,
tears,
cries of happiness and sadness,
joy and hate.

We are two in one,
making the other stronger,
better,
have a shared life.

Kids that we made,
history that we have,
a bond that's breaking but still holds firm,
for now, the two of us understanding the other,
less day by day….

The spark has gone,
passion only in arguments,
shouting,
no more love-making,
jubilating.

I have a girlfriend,
Safire is my infatuation,
electrification,
glorification in the wonder of another

With her spirit of youth,
freedom.
She's not weighed down with life,
duties of a wife,
but makes life worth living?

with her possibilities endless,
memories already had,
even more to make.

We know fun times,
not yet hard times,
now seeing how far we can stretch boundaries,
new realities.

We live,
love in the moment,

enjoy each other,
every day a surprise not the same,
not mundane,
not a bigger game.

She is not being wifey but my girl,

her vitality,
exuberance
who you once were;
I ask myself…
can she be my forever?

DIVORCE – THE TOUGHEST PHASE

Surely, even you dear reader, especially if you are in a faltering relationship, you question what's beyond the horizon and who could become your next fixation. Perhaps, with the passage of time and the process of maturing, I should remind myself that I am no longer a young and carefree individual, and that constant thoughts of sex should diminish... but that's exactly what I craved; shagging and intimate encounters became an addiction.

I can't stop replaying the entirety of my relationship with Grace. I scrutinize every screw-up, make a long list of all I did wrong and which ultimately led to its demise. I have compiled a list of all my wrongdoings. I take responsibility and accountability for all my fuck-ups and have put the list in a metaphorical box, this as I strive to take control rather than allowing my failings to incessantly invade my consciousness. It will be up to me when I lift the lid and analyse my mistakes, when to retake control and pursue a better self. I only hope Grace does the same as, so far, she has not admitted one grain of culpability! Everyone knows, that in a toxic relationship both sides make mistakes, whether significant or trivial.

I don't know what the future holds. Maybe it will be liberating to not have as many responsibilities. Yes, I will have to pay child maintenance and probably alimony, but I will be in a better state of mental health with not having somebody to be beholden to, someone controlling me. This was the cause of my greatest emotional distress. I can once again do what I want with no fear of upsetting anyone. It's a universal truth, that it's only those you love, your friends, that cause you the most hurt. By untangling myself of Grace, I've engineered a fresh start. I can now embark on a new journey of self-discovery and can re-emerge into the light with my head held high confident in my newfound identity. I know though this will not be a simple or painless process.

I wake not knowing what the day will bring.
I do know...
I will leave to a foreign field in four days,
I have a job interview in one hour,
that my wife will take the kids to school,
that my father is ill and I might not see him again,
that my marriage is hanging by a thread,
that my heart belongs to another...
Safire,
that is how my day starts.

Children school bound,
interview starts,

goes as well as can be expected,
work, a potential escape hatch from an impossible decision,
position I've been running from.

The day continues productively,
major project finally finished,
two months of self-motivation can now be directed elsewhere,
to the upcoming consultancy,
to my children,
to the woman of my lust.

Eat a nice dinner Grace cooked,
leave the house,
the missus not coming,
need to relieve my brain from the strain,
chat to friends on WhatsApp,
find people to talk in the flesh.

Text saucy messages with Safire,
drink pints,
chat to boring mountaineers,
go karaoke;
an ok evening,
one of my own design and making.

In good mood go home,
Internal conversations of sex with Grace forefront of my booze sozzled mind;
I must satisfy her to stop her bothering me,
the problem,
my body doesn't react,
I don't erect;
the mind willing,
the subconscious not so,
my dick staying Mr. Floppy,
this,
an accurate representation of this point on my time space continuum;

I fall into drunken slumber.

Wake,
thought last night ok if disappointing finish.

See messages on my phone…
sent to my lover…
but not by me,
my phone hacked,
this some spy shit!

Voice notes of hatred to my lover,
Safire,
by my wife;
holy fuck,
end of this life!

Safire,
spat.

Asshole,
wallop.

Cheating bastard,
said straight at my heart.

Fucker,
reiterated.

Cheater,
regurgitated.

I cower in hope,
punch.

Kick, slap,
relentless.

Kitchen,
where's the sink?

Look,
disarming.

Look,
contempt.

Look,
hatred.

Look…
no hope.

I can't take,
I love you one days,
insults and fists the next;
threats and then kisses,
stop manipulating me;
change is a coming,
I'm not sure where fate will take me.

I have to see my father,
maybe one last time.
My indiscretions not disclosed,
sleep on the couch.

Wake,
kids dispatched to school,
long relationship discussion ensues,
Grace calls my mum,
she emotionally vulnerable,
no dirty Safire details left out,
no sexual adventures hidden,
I'm banished from my parent's house,
forever.

Talk to brother,
write long email,
highlight there are always two sides to every story.

Stop holding the kids' happiness over me,
said to grace,
this outcome yours as much as mine;
there's always two sides to every story;
change is a coming,
I'm not sure where fate will take me.

Our marriage is miserable,
divorce the hardest change of all,
those who I fought so hard and so long for,
now I cave in.
Where will my next battle be?
as change is a coming,
I'm not sure where fate will take me.

Where did it all go wrong when there was so
much right?
We created now destroy,
those closest, collateral damage.

Our issues impact more than simply us,
three generations;
one together splits into more than two halves,
the parts less than the sum of the whole.

How do we move forward from this low point?
is there any chance of reconciliation,
an amicable split?

Will it be mutually assured destruction,
both using nuclear weapons to eviscerate,
evaporate,
cremate,
bludgeon and trample on the other's emotions.
refuse to commiserate (for what was good),
communicate (to find a way forward);
liberate will not feel as good if we don't accom-
modate.

Decisions,
the hardest of choices
must be made,
not constantly mind played.

We must wave goodbye to
love,
hello to uncertainty,
accountability for
repercussions,
life interruptions,
consequences for those most affected,
they not understanding,
comprehending,
maybe never forgiving
everybody though keeps on living.

Whether friend or foe,
the sun will shine and moon will wane,
the tide will come in and go out,
life will continue,
there will be a tomorrow but not the same as
yesterday,
with you.

Grace,
take me or leave me,
accept me or walk away;
love or hate me,
the choice is yours.

I'm not less of a person if I don't fit your idea of
whom I should be;
this, your problem.

Why a hater if you no longer know me?
You don't know my life,
what I've experienced,
what my influences are or what has made me, me;
worry about your life,
not mine.

I'm a lover not a fighter.
If you want to be friends,
great,

if not…
I will not only survive,
but thrive.

Your call to mum has pushed me to the very
limit,
my absolute,
into space,
countdown from ten then emotional blast off.

I control myself,
my tongue,
my natural inclinations and peccadillos,
but you keep pushing,
pushing,
pushing,
SNAP!

What do you expect?
Why are you a hypocrite?
What is reasonable,
justifiable,
liveable;
why do you still want more of me?

We are in a state of turmoil,
a forever war,
no armistice or negotiation,
no peace in our times…
for the good of our kids
for you and I,
why can't you be respectable?

if I had a level of understanding,
maybe I could understand,
you, the personification of no transparency.

I am so drained,
the positive force run out.
I'm left with nothing,
not even negative.
You have a lack of care,
of empathy.

Despite,
or maybe because I can see you in me,
I in you,
we have stayed together…
together we…
but you have a block,
a boulder you cannot break,
remove or detonate,
shift around to see any good in me.

I'm all that is bad in your life,
negative,
but I'm not the start and end of your problems;
I have much to offer to those willing to receive.

I don't know what else to say that's not already
been said,
so I will say nothing,
keep mute,
my words run dry,
my heart a closed gate,
I don't want to hate.

You are still a tornado,
you have crushed my volcano;
is this what you wanted?
This is not a way I can,
shall live,
this is not me,
a supplicant,
a pussy whip,
a person without direction,
conviction,
motivation.

Decide what you want if not me.
Let's stop this torturous dance,
bid adieu,
wish each other good luck,
decide what's best for the kids,
our lives forever entwined,
combined.

What started on the dance floor,
went via mountain top and wedding beach,

has gone full circle,
we real strangers,
no longer friends.

There is no thought of the other,
of what we have done together,
no willingness to the basics of friendships,
for the kids we have or life built.

Your disregard,
I'm nothing more to you,
no chance of a way forward,
no ability to look at the good,
not anything other than having your cake and
eating it.

I can't go on this way.
I need a minimum of friendship,
otherwise,
what's the point?
it can't be one rule for you another for me,
my soul not bulletproof.

You have made your decision.
I gave you keys to a new reality,
well…
too late.
I asked honesty,
being straightforward,
but such is life.

How do you do it?
Why do you do it?
Do you want peace or arguments?
Be friend or foe?

Words said so lightly,
vocalisations with unintended consequences,
you not thinking of the impact,

the potential boiling anger,
a red rage flowing through mind, soul and body.

You have a carelessness,
thoughtlessness,
a speak before thinkingness,
then surprised by consequence.

Your impulsiveness,
don't give a fuckedness,
leads to reaction,
manifestation,
emotion removing the rationale,
releasing the handbrake,
going full throttle to prove you wrong,
to spite you and your words,
to show two fingers and a dick that will be for
another chick.

So, good luck,
good night,
goodbye.

Don't look back in anger.

I loved you and you loved me,
but we have nothing left,
nothing to hold onto;
I've no chips left to play and you've called my
bluff.

I'm not afraid to take the tough,
rough decisions,
to be accountable for choices

to mature,
to own and be responsible for implementing
plans.

I thought together would be forever,
but now I'm alone,
forced apart by choices,
decisions.

There's no comfort or joy with you.
I have no one to snuggle up to when cold and
lonely,
talking nonsense and joking;
we are apart,
time now, pack suitcase and depart.

You're no longer the woman on my arm,
though will always be the love of my life;
I pray we can survive somehow,
for the sake of the kids;
I will always keep a candle in my heart for you.

You guided me through turbulent times,
you were my port in heaving seas,
the lighthouse to my depression,
the hope I wish I was to you.

Your forgiveness and understanding,
were my absolution,
your love and friendship,
my salvation,
but if you have no more love to give,
don't look back in anger for what you have
thrown away as it's enough,
it's enough,
let go of your mistrust,
stop hurting me,
us.

Let's live in peace and harmony,
friends, if not marital unity.

We are both angry and confused,
not knowing,
caring what the other wants.

Let's live in peace and harmony,
friends, if not marital unity.

We made love,
shagged in cars,
fields,
under trees,
in the sea,
shower,
tents and beds.

Let's live in peace and harmony,
friends, if not marital unity.

Our bodies were united,
words whispered,
coupling and canoodling.
Promises made,
experiences shared and hopes explored,
but now I'm rejected,
ejected from your life.

I'm angry and confused,
what do you want?
I'm not made of stone
and loving you hurts.

Let's live in peace and harmony,
friends, if not marital unity.

You sowed confusion,
apprehension through self-determination.
You have choices,
but you can't have it all;
decide priorities.

I'm angry and confused,
what do you want?
I'm not made of stone
and loving you hurts.

Let's live in peace and harmony,
friends, if not marital unity.

We're passing time
as time passes by.
We have loved and lost,
lost and loved.
We were a coming together,
intertwining,
failing and now parting.

Let's live in peace and harmony,
friends, if not marital unity.

It's enough,
it's enough,
let go of your mistrust.
Stop hurting me,
us.

Let's live in peace and harmony,
friends, if not marital unity.

Our hope,
love,
truth and friendship has ended like a candle in
the wind,
this,
before our marriage finished.

I cry for the pain in my heart,
I'm no longer a clown full of jokes and laughter,
Anything being possible,
my heart now stone,

devoid of expectation,
joy or freedom,
my thoughts now dark.

What hope do I have when I have no one to rely
on,
when no one has my back,
my best friend lies,
deceives,
manipulates,
makes my heart cry for the loss of dreams.

What sort of life is being separated from chil-
dren,
being in in an impossible position,
leading parallel lives?
This is a life of sadness,
reflection,
hopelessness,
of giving up on trust.

When someone puts their desires above the com-
mon good,
the family,
what sort of person are they?
Selfish?
Misunderstood?
Goal driven?
I don't know what to think...

For the first time I feel your honesty
that truth,
the end of us,
you revelling who you are,
you own ambitions,
sub-conscious taking priority,
priority over our family,
your children.

You have been playing with me,
us,
no intention of coming of hope
or love.

Hope,
love,
truth and friendship ended like
a candle in the wind,
this,
before our marriage finished.

I still love you,
I could psychologically destroy
you,
murder you,
cannibalise and spit you out...
this what you've driven me to.

You are,
were my everything,
the ying to my yang,
calm me like Buddha,
gives me meaning,
determination and anger.

You have so much hatred I could kill myself,
you,
all that we have built;
love is crazy shit!

Our love is now built on a lie,
falsehood,
deception,
misinformation
errant erection.

You thought it was love at first sight,
The truth,
I had a three-hole night,
a random bitch,
girl,
someone to try my luck,
fuck... again and again and again!

What were you to me?
A nice smile,
a pair of tits and a tight ass,
but who cares,
girls come and go,

all wanting something,
telling lies,
pretending they're honest.

I know the games women play
I've been played...
so this time let me be the player.

We talked,
chatted and still you wanted more,
it all.

I gave what I had but it was not enough...
so I took control,
a bus trip,
fuck trip,
meeting tomorrow,
I'm fucking tonight,
romantic holidays–
fuck that,
get some foreign pussy.

This is my life,
my control,
I will not be broken by you,
for you,
respect that or I will destroy you.

You who thinks she is so wonderful,
brilliant,
clever and friend to everyone,
but who is really so lonely,

used and mentally abused by your family…
why is that?

There is a falseness that runs though you,
you who can't face your demons,
pretends they don't exist with plastic smiles,
but dies within,
knowing the truth that no one loves you.

I'm the person who did,
who still does,
but you pushed me away,
destroyed what you had,
aiming for the moon,
the Hollywood marriage,
Instagram happiness,
but forgetting all that we had,
the small wins,
the big successes,
failures we overcame together...
but that was not enough.

If you want to play games,
I will destroy you as you killed me,
like you tried to kill yourself...
apparently,
a pill call for attention in front of kids...
the most selfish thing a parent could ever do,
ever,
ever!

I'm a griffin-
strong and daring as a tiger,
I lifted you on my wings.

You give me nothing,
no fun,
no daring or adventure,
no emotional or financial support,
no sex,
I only stayed out of a sense of duty to my children,
to my parents,
but this was still not enough,
you who wanted more than I could give,
it all.

I love you,
I despise you-
why can't I be your friend?
Why do you try to control the uncontrollable?

I prefer to be by myself than with you,
this is the truth.
I love you,
have moved mountains for you,
have wasted my time on you,
but you are really nothing to me,
I mentally stronger than you,
been through more fires.

I'm sure, you too are having internal conversation,
discourse,
your narrative,
that you're the heroine,
the victim…
guess what,
that's fake bullshit,
you living a fake dream,
time,
bitch,
for your ego to be punctured,
to hear the reality,
it was only my hope,
the cellotape that kept our family together,
no more,
you are about to reap what you sowed.

You bring nothing to my life,
why do I still call you my wife?
This,
legal absurdity,
so fuck you if it's war you want!

It has taken me 3 hours,
2 affairs,
yours and mine,
7 poems,
14 years to realise this,
to say,
fuck you!

I needed time and alcohol units,

poems to get my rhythm on,
and to say,
fuck you.

When I needed someone the most,
you,
my wife,
I thought for life,
we fought,
you pushed,
throwing spears every chance you had;
fuck you!

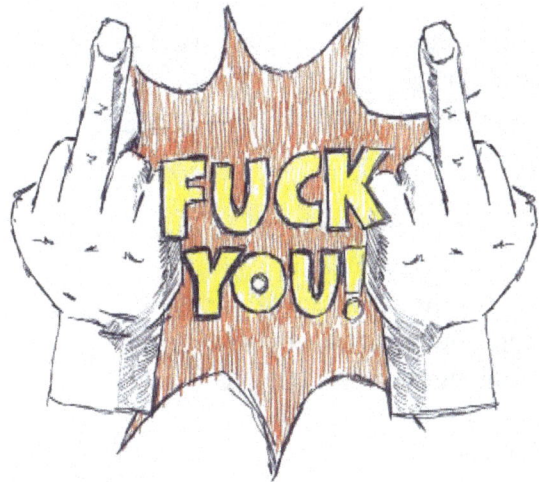

You're all about the manipulate,
not capitulate,
mind games,
thinking so clever…
but turning your biggest supporter against you;
fuck you!

We both made wrong,
why can't you admit,
what's it with your ego,
id,
that you will throw everything away,
rumble,
no show little humble?
Fuck you!

Turn kids against me,
their minds easier to change,
rearrange,
easier than my friends and family,

those projects failed!
Fuck you!

I loved you so much,
did everything for you,
no questions asked,
no demand made other than to be your friend,
you didn't,
couldn't give me anything;
fuck you!

No matter what you think you'll win,
we'll both lose,
you throwing it away on your avarice,
self-conceit,
this regretful deceit;
fuck you!

I'm not an angry person,
not how I was bought up.
Lucky for my advantages,
parents and persona,
you making me a worse man,
human being;
fuck you!

Good luck with what you do,
with your life.
We will always be joined,
kids tying us together,
but fuck you for breaking my heart,
fuck you for throwing everything we built togeth-
er away!

I will work life out myself;
fuck you!

You have won your bullshit,
mind full of shit game,
you becoming like the mother you hate,
the snake eating its tail!
Fuck you!

I know you internalising the same about me,
this natural,

but you been doing this for months,
years.

This fuck you is for you fucking us with your
jealousy,
Insecurity.
Fuck you!
Fuck you!
Fuck you!
Fuck you,
you fucking fuck!

I tried my best,
but this not good enough-
I'm done,
I'm done,
I'm outta here.

Don't know what else to do,
if you don't even want friendship-
I'm done,
I'm done,
I'm outta here.

We can have open lives,
but I can't take your closed heart-
I'm done,
I'm done,
I'm outta here.

What more do you want,
that I can't give?
I'm done,
I'm done,
I'm outta here.

Be straightforward,
that's all I ask.
I'm done,
I'm done,
I'm outta here.

This is it
no more playing me like a fool.
I'm done,

I'm done,
I'm outta here.

Gave you freedom,
my heart,
but that not enough.
I'm done,
I'm done,
I'm outta here.

I need something from you...
that you can't,
won't give.
I'm done,
I'm done,
I'm outta here.

This is life,
no more words to be said.
I'm done,
I'm done,
I'm outta here.

You and I will survive,
apart,
not together thrive.
I'm done,
I'm done,
I'm outta here.

I cry for lost hope,
I pray for your happiness.
I'm done,
I'm done,
I'm outta here.

I need change,
to look after my mental health.
I'm done,
I'm done,
I'm outta here.

Tear myself to sleep,
even though so much joy in the world.
I'm done,
I'm done,
I'm outta here.

Have your boyfriend,
but if you can't find space for me,
I'm done,
I'm done,
I'm outta here.

I'm not the idiot you think,
I cry tears of a clown.
I'm done,
I'm done,
I'm outta here.

Live your dreams,
I no longer in them.
I'm done,
I'm done,
I'm outta here.

This is it!
I'm sad for what was once great,
for the hope we once had,
for all we did together
for not finding a way forward.
I'm done,
I'm done,
I'm done,
I'm done,
I'm done,
I'm done,
I'm done,
I'm done,
I'll sign divorce papers and then I'm outta here.

THE, FINDING A WAY FORWARD PHASE

And so it happened, the divorce papers were signed. My love for Grace morphed to familiarity, banality, boredom, contempt, anger, hatred… and I've gone full-circle back to singleton, such is the life journey. Now is time for new beginnings. I must take charge of my life no matter the slings and arrows that will be fired my way (from Grace and my kids). I will summon bravery, stoicism and find solutions. I aspire to find a like-minded companion, a fellow life pirate, so that when I look back I can honestly proclaim, that I have no regrets. Carpe Diem. That I have lived temet nosce. And now, I ponder the question: what should I do next? How can I find a woman who can positively transform my life, turn me from frog to prince? Guide me on living for the now rather than dwelling on past mistakes and broken hearts? I yearn for a love without limitations or expectations. Someone who will not hide their darkest secrets, worry in silence and conceal their fears and indiscretions under a veneer of respectability. I desire a partner who can be a listening ear and offer wise counsel. Who will hear and speak words of wisdom, each syllable striking a note, every word resonating with a mixture of regret for the past and hope and joy for the future.

I acknowledge the regrets I carry from times gone by, while embracing the hope for what lies ahead and what is possible. I will keep my heart and mind open to the endless possibilities.

I'm in a funk,
hard decisions been and gone,
the end of an era,
I sadly reflect.

Words exchanged,
the axis of worlds forever altered.
That is life,
the passing of seasons the same as the movement
of emotions,
a constant state of flux,
life swinging to new rhythms.

My heart is broken but simultaneously overjoyed,
my love,

my North Star,
my Grace has turned into the women I always
thought she could be,
would be,
knew she had the potential to be.

It's a shame this was the signal,
the end of us,
our marriage,
soulmates no more.

I will always love her,
she is my number one,
but I am no more for her;
this happens.

I must be stoical,
accepting,
understanding and move forward.

This will be the last time I'm serious with a wom-
an,
if I couldn't make it work with Grace,
it will never happen;
I can't put myself through such heartbreak again.
I, a forever wanderer in life and love as the sea-
sons pass.

Even in Spring,
time of rebirth,
hope and longer days.
I see people walking by,
freedom in their steps,
in their souls.
But, I'm stuck in my life,
not sure which way forward,
which way back.

Summer comes.
I'm frigid from the air con and sweat on the
commute.
Iced veins for my ex,
Grace,
lost passion for my lover,
Safire.
I'm stuck in an office,
pointless meetings passing the time,
as I see people walking by freedom in their steps,
in their souls.

Here comes the Autumn,
wind and rain,
long nights and sodden shoes.
Depression,
loneliness sets in.
I think of searching for escape though don't have
the courage,
this, as I see people walking by,
freedom in their steps,
in their souls.

It's Winter,
I feel no sun on my skin,
warmth in my heart.
There is no joy from my self-imposed exile,
no Christmas presents from my kids.
I have little motivation to keep living,
all the while I see people walking by,
freedom in their steps,
in their souls.

I know not what to do.
I have loved and lost,
lost and loved,
this is life,

a coming together,
intertwining of lives and parting of ways.

I have been in love,
lust,
life taking me elsewhere.
Desire for Grace,

Safire,
not enough to keep us together.

I have been loved,
lusted
but my desire to go elsewhere
stronger than to keep us together.

In cars,
fields,
under trees and in the sea,
shower,
tents and bed,
bodies united,

Words were whispered.
panting expired,
coupling and canoodling as promises made
experiences shared,
hopes explored.

A life is more worth living with someone riding
high,
pinned on their side.
Now I know not what to do,
no longer know who I am
as I wander city to city,
bed to bed,
lie to lie,
not sure what the next week,
day or hour will bring.

I no longer have a drive,
a motivation,
a sense of purpose to move my life forward.

When I wake,
I turn to.my right…
no one there,
no one to hold me tight,
hear my hopes,
fears and desires.

I eat,
sleep,

repeat,
not caring what makes hours tick by.

When I turn to the left I see unpacked suitcases
and a dying plant,
more tree that big it is,
I, to slovenly to feed it water,
its leaves dying like me;
what sadness,
a weeping analogy.

So, I people watch,
individuals,
couples,
families,
friends,
acquaintances old and new,
chatting,
joking,
laughing and enjoying each other's company
while I consider my loneliness in this world,
cast adrift.

What fate holds in store,
I don't know,
no one can.

I realise,
only I will ever have my back.

I am the only person I can rely on,
who will not leave or let me down,
lie to me.

It is only I that can decide my future,
decide who I share this life with;
I will be the last man standing at my O.K Coral
shooting till I run dry.

But I can't get rid of you,
Grace
My North Star,
you're a ghost in my heart.

We are not together in this
tangible world,
but you are in my dreams,
a ghost in my heart.

I think of kissing your lips,
holding your hips,
running my hand through your hair,
sharing jokes under duvet.

We had life and love together,
a future of hope,
excitement and courage to overcome,
the world ours to fashion;
now you're a ghost in my heart,
I not willing to accept the truth,
you are gone,
never to return,
our love forever broken.

I can't exorcise you,
my life,
ex-wife,
you who were my everything,
my reason for being,
my motivation to get out of bed,
to do the work I didn't enjoy,
but now you've gone;
your ghost haunts my heart.

I write this poem on a train,

the real world.
It's been a day of joy and laughter;
lunch with aunt,
beers with the lads.

I enter the carriage,
carefree and a little tipsy,
my eye chances on you,
you with the boyfriend that you denied,
lied,

now I see you have his heart tied to you,
you who were my everything,
my hope,
my one time,
my got swallowed and spat out,
my relationship fucked,
my happened,
now you're my obsession,
revolution,
as loving you was my identification,
inflation,
now bastardisation,
hate infliction,
suicide nation.
no longer salvation and gentrification.

You,
who prey on my,
played with my emotion,
caused me commotion,
eyes welling with rejection,

utter dejection,
combustible hatetration,

Good luck to him,
you.
I will make new words that are free-flowing,
but spewing out you who killed me and finished
worlds.

I return to empty flat
twenty floors up,
the world before me;
there is life in this one view…
but I feel in the basement.
I see fire in candles,
passion through
windows,
light and hope,
cheer and good
times around…
but I have ice in my
veins,
depression,
fears and regrets in
my head,
hopelessness in my
heart;
I'm constricted in claustrophobia and feel en-
closed in a life without you.

I have perfect clarity,
everything possible to others…
but not to me.
I could take a chance and twist,
but I choose to stick,
preferring the safe to unknown,
solitude rather than the vagaries of love.

I prefer to be unhappy and trust the familiar,
than try the new,
think reignite passions with you,
Grace,
the ghost in my heart.

As I look over the world,
my future from twenty floors up,

I stare at my phone,
waiting to hear your voice,
your laughter;
your love,
your lullaby;
I know it will not come.

I remember how two became one,
I was Adam and you Eve,
but it's no more;
I lost you,
and then you lost me.

We still have love
but live separate lives;
we can't change the past but can move forward
together.

Your strength of mind and purpose,
beauty of soul and body,
love of others...
is what attracted me to you.

We want individual peace,
but miss our noise;
we want together,
but value independence.

Your strength of mind and purpose,
beauty of soul and body,
love of others...
is what attracted me to you.

You are an ex-wife,
mother,
no longer lover,
but everyone also needs a best friend,
someone to share romantic dinners and dirty
weekends,
wild nights and lazy Sundays.

Your strength of mind and purpose,
beauty of soul and body,
love of others...
is what attracted me to you.

Time has passed since we first met.
We have grown older,
understand life and ourselves more,
better.
Our personalities have changed,
we're no longer who we first met,
we respect the others current needs and wants.

Your strength of mind and purpose,
beauty of soul and body,
love of others...
is what attracted me to you.

You need friends,
work fulfilment,
financial independence,
feeling loved and needed…
as much as I.

Your strength of mind and purpose,
beauty of soul and body,
love of others...
is what attracted me to you.

I want to be a giver and receiver of presents,
of planning surprises and being wowed.
Having exhilarations not pre-conditions,
limitations.
Living for the moment,
not always abiding by rules.
Accepting mistakes and understanding we're
human,
irrational,
passionate and instinctive.

Your strength of mind and purpose,
beauty of soul and body,
love of others...
is what attracted me to you

We have much together:
our kids
a willingness to do whatever it takes,
So, let's build on our strengths and understand-
ing,
once more us against the world rather than each
other.
We should rejoice in the other's happiness,
in accomplishments achieved individually and
together,
of both living as free birds.

Your strength of mind and purpose,
beauty of soul and body,
love of others...
is what attracted me to you.

I want you to be free,
free with yourself,
with other lovers.

Your strength of mind and purpose,
beauty of soul and body,
love of others...
is what attracted me to you.

What I want most of all is happiness....
yours,
our kids,
mine.
If we can accommodate,
understand rather than fight,
argue,
compromise,
then two can still be more powerful than one.

Your strength of mind and purpose,
beauty of soul and body,
love of others...
is what attracted me to you.

Two can still be together
but in a new configuration…
each respecting,
rejoicing in the other;
two complementary halves rather than one
whole.

Your strength of mind and purpose,
beauty of soul and body,
love of others...
is what still attracts me to you.

Divorce is horrible times,
hard times,
miserable conversations…
but soon new chapters to be written,
life to live.

Relationships,
I'm done with them.
I will live to my own rules and accountabilities,
more children not in the equation,
vasectomy the best option.

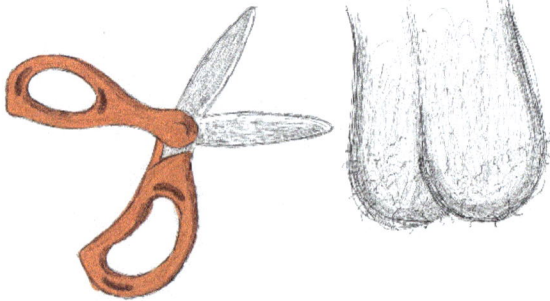

I have 4 kids that I love,
would do anything for;
they are my pride and joy,
but no more would I want.

I will go back into the world and see what the
tide brings in.
Chat to friends,
seek solace,
keep an open mind open to wise words and new
hearts.

We meet,
start chat.
Tea not beer,
no fireworks explode,
but happy times,
good times,
start to feel my life living to a new rhyme with
you,
Jessica.

You tell me,
life,
full of shit,
people,
those you thought were friends,
lovers,
partners till the end of days,
let you down,
deceive,
lie,
emotionally and physically abuse you.

You feel worthless,
a nothing,
no good,
a miserable wreck that no one will love.

You get hit,
beaten,
but go back for more shit,
your insecurities deceiving,
that one day they will love you,
the way you love them,
worship then,
their word, your command,
their word making you their sexual deviant,
someone you don't want to be…
but you relent,
give in,
anything to feel their love,
to hear their whisper,
for them to kiss your neck,
lick between your legs,
make you laugh like a love-struck teenager,
anything to see them pleased.

That was me,
a damsel in distress,
a wilted flower,
a bunch of other idioms.

I have more life scratches than a kitty,
then a humongous tiger could inflict,
then I said:

FUCK,
THAT,
SHIT!

I got up,
put my boxing gloves on,
told him to shut the fuck up and took control.

My success,
telling him, get outta my life!
I don't won't your negativity,
I'm royalty!

My advice...
be a bad ass,
life kick ass.

Experience,
a hard teacher,
time a good healer.

You have shone light into my darkness,
now I have choices:
stay as I am or take a chance on me,
on you,
Jessica,
my Athena.

Experience,
a hard teacher,
time a good healer.

What happens if you go?
I will have nothing left,
nothing to hold onto.

Experience,
a hard teacher,
time a good healer.

You say,
"Trust me.
Go for it.
Just do it.
I love you and you love me."

Experience,
a hard teacher,
time a good healer.

I close my eyes,
say a little prayer like Aretha told us,
and hope my lottery numbers are called;
I'll go swimming for my dreams with you.

Experience,
a hard teacher,
time a good healer.

The roll of my life now in your hands,
your hands that are holding my life,
my life that is now entwined in yours;
our love that will decide fates.

Experience,
a hard teacher,
time a good healer.

This is a new kinda love
The future in front,
past behind,
living for the now,
living for you.

You are now the one who gives me courage,
hope and love;
love that I need,
a friendship I desire,
crave.

You are my companion that heals wounds,
I can be your nurse.
Together,
we are two in one,
can hope for a brighter tomorrow,
for a life together,
forever.

You are my mate who can see into my soul.
my reflection of self,
a fellow life pirate.
We are humpty dumpty and can put each other
together again,
there's no need for all the king's men…

just each other,
hope and love.

A FINAL THOUGHT

I tried my best, although I must admit that I'm not a particularly honourable person; I make no bones about that. I have not done great deeds or been exceptional. I was living an ordinary life until someone extraordinary came into my world and turned it upside down. Grace turned the mundane into the unforgettable. She taught me how it's better to nurture curiosity than live in ignorance. That one should live without prejudice. That it is fine to observe and make up your own mind rather than have predefined expectations. That you should always question the obvious. For my part, I hope she now realises that it's never a question of right or wrong, good or bad, black or white, but a million shades in-between; it's all about context.

I will forever remember Grace fondly no matter how it all went down, the messy ending. Now, I have a new opportunity to build a life with someone by my side. I no longer have a North Star; instead, I have an Athena. Jessica represents my future, and only time will reveal what lies ahead.

Having gone through the gamut of relationship emotions, here's my take on the secret sauce, the magic formula of a long and loving relationship.

1. Be attracted to each other's mind, body and soul.
2. Appreciate their good and bad, both their devil and the angel, their strengths and temptations; everyone is human. Your partner is not like you, they do not think like you; that's cool, accept them as they are.
3. Constantly show love and respect.
4. Be forgiving.
5. If you cheat, lie or in any other way betray your beloved, do it in such a way so as not to demean them.
6. Even when things are shitty– and there will be times– resist the urge to leave.
7. Kids need parents.
8. No one wants to grow old alone.
9. Love is a devotion to an ideal not reality. Understand this truth, it helps with lessening disappointment.
10. Believe what you have together is more than apart.
11. Be honest and accepting of honesty.
12. Trust and talk to your partner; if you don't, separation is an inevitability.
13. A biggie– leave your phone, laptop of any other device out of the bedroom. This is your sanctuary as a couple; don't let distractions intrude.
14. You should try to surprise them every now and then. Birthdays, Christmas, and anniversaries are a good chance to show that you are thinking of them.
15. And now for the big one… if you sort out and discuss, nurture a satisfying sex life, share a real honesty and have regular intimacy, you will likely be

RULES
— FOR A HAPPY —
MARRIAGE
LAUGH TOGETHER
be the first to say I'm sorry
say i love you
FORGIVE
DON'T BRING UP THE PAST
communicate & trust
HUG HOLD HANDS · KISS
be in the moment
remember why you fell in love
COMPLIMENT EACH OTHER
LISTEN
encourage each other
show gratitude

happier in other parts of your relationship. Conversely, if one partner is sexually frustrated, it may manifest in various exasperations, potentially leading to infidelity. Think about it. In a long-term relationship, passion inevitably withers and is replaced by domesticity, adventure by security, connection with the need for separation and awareness of own needs. Relationships are paradoxical. In a world where we expect everything easily, instant gratification is expected. We don't just want to be happy but happier than we could ever possibly be, and certainly happier than our peers. And if one party is dissatisfied, they are just one swipe away from finding a new lover. This is the polar opposite to back in the day when marriages were often rooted in duty more than love.

16. Everyone has a different past. Give your partner freedom to be their true self in the knowledge that your best friend is always there for you.

17. Share new experiences in life, laughter and love together.

18. As for marriage... I bet when you were growing up you watched cartoons or read stories where the main narrative revolved around falling in love and living happily ever after. This notion is reinforced throughout our life from advertisements, laws, tax-breaks and societal expectations. However, the reality is that endings are rarely happy if you're not willing to be flexible with the one you love.

Thank you, dear reader, my friend for being on this poetic journey. I hope through my experiences I have given you a new perspective on life. So, I say, never blame your circumstances. A positive mind-set will always lead to a more fortuitous outcome than a negative approach. One should not fear failure; it happens– get up and give it another lash. Don't be ashamed of your mistakes; learn from them. We all screw-up, accept this is part of life. Embrace experience, good or bad; there is always something to be learned. If you don't go after what you want, you will never have it. If you don't ask, the answer is always no. If you don't step forward, you will remain in the same place. Be curious and have a willingness to engage with the unknown. Questioning does not show weakness but is rather a sign of strength, a true measure of intelligence. Open yourself to the world and express that you aren't afraid to exhibit your ignorance but want to learn, search for knowledge and truth from those who can educate and guide. "By doubting we are led to question, by questioning we arrive at the truth." Peter Abelard, 1079– 1142

I love you,
we are here together;
nothing can break us,
destroy us nor get in our way.

You're the one who knows,
understands,
comprehends and gets me.
The person I can be my true self with is you,
I hope,
pray, I'm that one for you

My grey hairs spreading faster than my expanding waistline,

receding hairline,
shortening lifeline.

As I get older,
I hope not to be jealous of my younger self.

I won't accept the creaks and groans that are
becoming more frequent,
the once fresh feeling of life now becoming stale
as my eyes dimming,
teeth rotting and cancer approaching,
but I will keep on dancing,
living the life fandango.

You,
my friend,
lover,
sister from another mister,
are what gives me hope,
to start the day ahead.

Your freshness of youth allows me to forget my
soon goodbyes.

You allowed me to live again,
to be excited and feel exciting,
to live free minded,
unencumbered when in your arms.

I was...
where you are now
you will be...
where I am.
but till then,
I will not retire,
give up and flake out.

You gave me the desire to fight the dying of the
light and make me envious of the years we didn't
know each other.

THE END

ABOUT THE AUTHOR

I'm an entrepreneur & business consultant by day, novelist & poet by night. The son of a British Army officer, I volunteered in rural Tanzania in 1997 before going to university to study marketing. I have lived and worked in Ethiopia, Germany, Kenya, Jordan, Ireland, Malawi, Saudi Arabia, Tanzania and the UK over the last 25 years, my varied experiences of culture, relationships, food, music and everything else that makes the world go round, the source of my inspiration.

www.ingramcontent.com/pod-product-compliance
Lightning Source LLC
Chambersburg PA
CBHW081552040426
42448CB00016B/3297